HOMESCHOOL
HACKS

HOMESCHOOL
HACKS

HOW *to* GIVE YOUR KID
a GREAT EDUCATION
WITHOUT LOSING YOUR JOB
{ *or* YOUR MIND }

LINSEY KNERL

Tiller Press

New York   London   Toronto   Sydney   New Delhi

TILLER PRESS

An Imprint of Simon & Schuster, Inc.
1230 Avenue of the Americas
New York, NY 10020

First Tiller Press trade paperback edition April 2021

TILLER PRESS and colophon are trademarks of Simon & Schuster, Inc.

For information about special discounts for bulk purchases, please contact Simon & Schuster Special Sales at 1-866-506-1949 or business@simonandschuster.com.

The Simon & Schuster Speakers Bureau can bring authors to your live event. For more information or to book an event, contact the Simon & Schuster Speakers Bureau at 1-866-248-3049 or visit our website at www.simonspeakers.com.

Interior design by Laura Levatino

Manufactured in the United States of America

1   3   5   7   9   10   8   6   4   2

Library of Congress Cataloging-in-Publication Data
Names: Knerl, Linsey, author.
Title: Homeschool hacks : how to give your kid a great education without losing your job (or your mind) / by Linsey Knerl.
Description: First Tiller Press trade paperback edition. | New York : Tiller Press, 2021. | Includes bibliographical references.
Identifiers: LCCN 2020056601 (print) | LCCN 2020056602 (ebook) | ISBN 9781982171155 (paperback) | ISBN 9781982171186 (ebook)
Subjects: LCSH: Home schooling—United States.
Classification: LCC LC40 .K59 2021 (print) | LCC LC40 (ebook) | DDC 371.04/2—dc23
LC record available at https://lccn.loc.gov/2020056601
LC ebook record available at https://lccn.loc.gov/2020056602

ISBN 978-1-9821-7115-5
ISBN 978-1-9821-7118-6 (ebook)

For Sam,
and the eighteen years of bedtime stories
you never once complained about reading

CONTENTS

HOMESCHOOL
HACKS

{ *Introduction* }

HOW TO USE THIS BOOK

If you've picked up this book (or maybe received it as a gift), you're already homeschooling—or at least strongly considering it. Maybe, like so many parents who found their educational support system crumbling during COVID-19, you had previously assumed home education wasn't for you, especially if you were happy with your school. Or maybe it's been percolating for a while—an issue with bullying, lack of personalized special ed resources, or a general feeling that there's something better out there.

However you came here, I'm glad. This book was written to welcome all homeschoolers and those who want to know how to support their homeschooling friends and family. The COVID-19 pandemic has certainly brought new attention to a method of learning that had already been growing in popularity. The observations and advice in this book can be applied by both those who are brand-new to homeschooling and those who have been doing it for years. These tips will work for lifers (those who plan on taking it from K–12) as well as those just trying to get through the semester. And I hope they can also help explain why homeschooling works, so you can share them with grandparents or family members who want to play an active role in helping your children succeed but aren't really sure how.

Why me for this book? I've been homeschooling for well over fifteen years. In fact, it's the only way my kids have been educated. In 2007, I began writing. It started as a hobby, then became a side gig, and finally blossomed into a full-time career. Just a couple of years later, my husband's career was a casualty of the recession, and we decided to put all our energy into establishing our homestead and growing my business. And it's a good thing we did, too. While it's had its ups and downs, the writing business has not only supported our six kids but given us the opportunity to watch them grow up close.

Has it been easy? Absolutely not. In fact, I never try to sell homeschooling as the easy choice. Like most of the decisions we've made based on our values or our goals for our family, it's been very hard at times. Homeschooling while running a business has sometimes made me feel like I'm not doing either one particularly well. On my worst days, I worry that I'm not spending enough time working with the kids. I also see how some of my peers are making more money than I am because they can spend all day writing books or selling pitches or producing podcasts. It's so hard not to compare ourselves to others; it's a natural human response to any challenging scenario.

So what drives us to keep at it, even though it's a difficult balance? While I can't always say that my business is better off for our homeschooling, I can say that our homeschool days (and my kids in general) are better off because of our business. Here are just a few of the highlights:

- My daughter, infant son, and I got to explore New York City as part of a media tour. We experienced the parks, museums, and food while I built industry relationships. (This daughter will be graduating college with a degree in media studies soon.)

- My son celebrated his sixteenth birthday on a plane en route to a conference where I was speaking in Washington, DC. We saw the National Archives up close before visiting our state senator's office and finished with a tour of the Justice Department. (This son is finishing high school with a desire to learn more about law.)

- Our entire family drove to North Dakota for a workshop I taught, stopping along the way for picnics in small parks, views of buffalo, and incredible photo opportunities of the Badlands. (Is there anything better for a lesson in geology than seeing these majestic rock structures in person?)

Over the years, I've spoken at dozens of events. I've covered hundreds of news stories. I've shared thousands of product reviews in my blog posts. And I've had my kids with me every step of the way. I nursed babies in the back of board meetings and taught lesson plans in car rentals and took my older kids to catered dinners while teaching them how to behave around tiny food plates. All these life lessons couldn't have happened if we didn't have the business, and if my husband and I weren't determined to use it to help them see more of the world.

We've always done our best to show our kids how hard work and an honest business can present new and exciting opportunities. They've also seen how times can be tough when you're self-employed. They know about taxes and working on weekends and that Mom and Dad are the ones who pay for the M&Ms in the hotel mini bar (so don't touch!). They see the fruits of our labor every day, from when I'm working on deadline with an article at 2 a.m. to when my husband lugs home the groceries and lumber for a DIY project at the end of every week. They've watched me cry while recovering from my sixth cesarean section while working up the energy to call a source about an upcoming story and helped Dad create amazing soups and sauces in our kitchen to keep me nourished. They see the delicate ecosystem that business owners like us maintain every day. It's been amazing.

• • •

Whether you read the book straight through or start with the chapters that speak directly to your current situation, I encourage you to give every section a try at some point. I've done my best to share universally applicable truths so that single parents can find common ground with married couples and civilians can find inspiration from those serving our country, for example.

I'm grateful for the opportunity to interview so many parents about their journeys. While I'll never know what it's like to be assigned to a different state for military duty, I learned a lot about how to handle moving (including what not to put in those boxes) from my military friends. Likewise, families who had nannies to help out or parents in urban areas with access to oh-so-many sports and hobbies shared unique stories that helped me assess what I'm doing for my own family.

Of course, there are also unlimited topics parents can disagree on when it comes to raising kids. From what to feed them to how long they should have a pacifier, it seems like nothing is settled. I understand these convictions; we all want only the best for our kids. If you're reading this book, you may be thinking that homeschooling is one of the ways to do it.

And it does have many advantages—chief among them the freedom to parent the way you want. You can ensure your child soaks up the good values you want instilled while also acquiring the necessary skills to face the ever-changing future. You don't have to wait for school boards or curriculum advisors or learning plans to be approved. You can, right now, do what you know is good for your child.

Of course, like anything worthwhile, it's not easy. Read through and take notes; it can be a bumpy ride, but one you'll never regret taking.

Chapter 1

WHO ARE THE HOMESCHOOLERS?

aking the decision to homeschool is like joining a club. So who's already in it? I can't answer specifically for your part of the world, as homeschoolers are as varied and unique as the reasons they've selected home education. Below are some examples. Do you see yourself in these stats?

The National Center for Education Statistics (NCES) shared that in 2016 the number of homeschooled students in the US totaled 1.69 million children, or 3.3 percent of the student population. This was a significant increase from the 850,000 students (1.7 percent) who were homeschooling in 1999.[1]

Homeschoolers are diverse and becoming more so every year. When the NCES last tracked ethnicity, culture, and race among homeschoolers in 2016, the data revealed:

- White homeschooled students made up 3.8 percent of the total student population, closely followed by Hispanic (3.5 percent), Black (1.9 percent), and Asian (1.4 percent).

- More children in rural areas are homeschooled than in cities, with 4.4 percent of these kids receiving a home education versus 3 percent of their urban peers. Even fewer suburban families made this choice; only 2.9 percent of these children were homeschooled.

- The big-family homeschool myth may not be without merit. The stats show that households with three or more children (4.7 percent) were more likely to homeschool than those with just one (2.7 percent) or two (2.3 percent) children.

- Two-parent homes showed a slightly greater share than single-parent homes. Just 2.3 percent of single-parent households made this choice, compared to 3.7 percent of those with two parents in the home. Surprisingly, 2 percent of the homeschool population had no parents in the home; they were being raised by relatives or friends.

However, these numbers don't tell the whole story of the "why" behind the choice. None of us go into home education with the idea that it's easier or cheaper, so why do we do it? Just look at the reasons parents in the 2016 data credited for making the leap:

- Environmental concerns, such as their children being exposed to drugs, negative peer pressure, or threats of violence, were cited by 34 percent of parents.
- Dissatisfaction with academics was listed for 17 percent of those homeschooling.
- The desire to educate according to their own faith or religion was the reasoning behind 16 percent of the parents asked by NCES.

Those weren't the only reasons, however—just the biggest. Slightly less than 6 percent of parents listed their child's special needs, including emotional and physical health, as the motivator. Moral instruction and a desire for a nontraditional school experience were also listed.

Parents are more likely to homeschool in the later grades. First- through third-grade homeschool students made up 2.4 percent of the US student population, while in the ninth through twelfth grades, homeschoolers increased to 3.8 percent. Whether parents felt those environmental issues to be more pressing at an older age or found more supplemental resources available for ninth- through twelfth-grade kids, the perception that homeschoolers teach only when the kids are little has been debunked by the data. Even if some parents feel less equipped to homeschool in the high school years, they're certainly doing it.

DISTANCE LEARNING VS. HOMESCHOOLING

While many public schools have offered distance learning (also called remote learning) for some of their students over the past decade, the wider embrace of distance learning didn't occur until the COVID-19 pandemic. Many parents who wouldn't normally have chosen to have their kids learn at home found themselves doing just that. These parents didn't necessarily object to their schools' curricula or policies or worry for their children's safety (other than in the face of COVID-19). Their kids were learning at home, but they weren't technically homeschooling.

However, the two ideas have a couple of important elements in common:

1. freedom to learn from anywhere with a computer and internet connection.
2. in some cases, the ability to flexibly schedule some coursework around your family obligations or personal obstacles.

I should stress that the second point is more variable. Many schools now require students to sit in front of the computer and learn along with everyone else in their class. This "live" learning method is also called "synchronous" learning or "Zoom schooling," after the video technology that many of the schools use.

WHY HOMESCHOOLING IS NOT SIMPLY DISTANCE LEARNING

I have many friends who are terrific parents, who love their kids, and who use the state-provided online learning platform. They also consider themselves homeschoolers because their kids learn at home—and, to be honest, they do play an active role in getting their kids logged on and doing their homework.

But here's how homeschooling is unique:

1. As the parent, you get to pick the curriculum and courses.
2. You can set the schedule, including the days you teach and how long you learn at each session.
3. You can add new courses that interest you, at any moment, without approval from anyone else (in most states).
4. You can do the teaching, or choose someone else to teach through tutoring, online courses, videos, or co-op classes.

You can also choose to ditch the online learning option completely. It's possible, even today, to homeschool with just books, workbooks, field trips, and DVDs. In fact, it's possible—and common—to homeschool with no computer at all. This is usually not an option for remote learning through a public or private school.

Sounds pretty good, right? But I wouldn't be leveling with you if I didn't admit that there are some challenges that come with homeschooling, too. These obstacles are worth evaluating before you decide if homeschooling is right for your family:

1. You are solely responsible for your child's learning outcomes.
2. You have to fund all materials, courses, and resources.
3. You may face discouragement from your family, friends, and school about your choice.

It's good to know what you're getting into, but don't let these obstacles stop you from exploring home education. They're struggles we've all gone through, and with more and more families choosing an independent and personalized approach to education, there are more support groups and resources than ever. Now is a great time to explore how life-changing homeschooling can be.

In the following chapters we'll look at why being responsible for your child's learning outcomes may be the best thing for your child—and for you. We'll discover the ways you can prioritize homeschooling in your schedule and finance those teaching tools you need to succeed. We'll also get into the stories of people, like you, who have gone out and blazed the homeschooling trail in their families and communities, even in the face of significant pushback.

If you're brand-new to homeschooling, these first steps can inspire you to continue on your path. If you've been homeschooling for a while, you can hopefully take away some tips you haven't discovered or be encouraged to reach out to other home educators with the same values and priorities you have. Since I've seen virtually every kind of family succeed at homeschooling, I'm confident your challenges, while unique, aren't insurmountable.

You can do this.

{ *Chapter 2* }

HOW DO YOU START?

hroughout the more than fifteen years that I've been home-schooling my six kids, I've gotten many questions from family and friends. Some are hoping to sniff out inadequacies in my methods or catch me in the act of not knowing what I'm doing. Others are honestly looking for answers. But I tell them all the same thing.

My goal is to give you enough step-by-step, actionable information to be able to start homeschooling tomorrow morning, if you wish. But before I explain exactly how it's done, I ask that you keep in mind one vital truth as you read this book (and any others you may have sitting on your shelf).

It probably won't be like you think.

Remember the first time you tried to feed your baby solid food? You were so excited that you spent hours in the gourmet baby food aisle, choosing between organic peas or a lovely sweet potato–prune mix. You purchased the ergonomic-handled spoon, a bib that catches crumbs at the bottom, and the most versatile high chair on the market.

How do you feed your baby? It's easy, you think. Open the jar, scoop up some puree, and place the food in the infant's open mouth. What could be simpler?

And then you try it. The puree is runnier than you thought; it dribbles down your hand and arm, leaving little on the spoon for the baby, who has shut her tiny mouth well before you get there anyway. Now the game has changed. All those "simple" directions still matter, but you must improvise your way from one step to the next. Singing a song to get your baby to smile so you can sneak a spoonful of puree in before he realizes what's happening and spits it all out onto his new bib? That's the truth that won't be completely covered in the book. That's the part that will require intuition, trust, and patience.

You are a parent. You have instincts, and you know your child better than anyone. That's the true advantage to you as a teacher, and why homeschooling can work so beautifully when done correctly. Every other homeschool parent has managed to fill in these gaps, and you will, too.

How? I abide by two rules when trying to brainstorm ways to get through these in-between steps:

1. We can try any methods possible if they're legal, safe, and follow the values of my family.
2. If the children are moving forward, they're learning, and homeschooling is considered a success.

If those seem vague or allow for too much flexibility, think back to those first few bites of baby food. I wasn't in your kitchen at the time, so I can't see if you played Taylor Swift or stood on your head or ate half a jar yourself to set an example. But if your methods followed rule number one and led to rule number two, you did a fine job. And that's how homeschooling will work.

THE FIRST STEPS TO STARTING YOUR HOMESCHOOL

Now that you can relax a bit, knowing that you have what it takes to parent your child through a quality education, what to do first? Since education is largely localized, your state and district requirements will be unique. The paperwork needed to homeschool in upstate New York, for example, will be quite different from what it takes to get started in Nebraska. From there, however, the methods are generally the same.

1. Research the Requirements for Your State

Start this process now, even if you aren't sure you want to start homeschooling until next year. Some states have a lot of hoops to jump through, paperwork to fill out, and permissions to grant. If you live in one of these states, it can take months to get from the research phase to your child's very first day in their homeschool environment. Make sure you're researching the most up-to-date information for your state as well, since laws change often. (Be sure to check out Chapter 3, with even more information on the legalities of homeschooling. Parents who share custody or who have unique family situations may need to reach out to an expert for legal advice.)

Where can you go for help? Home education support groups are the best way, and these can be found online through social media groups, websites, and sometimes even your state Department of Education. Find someone who has homeschooled within the last year (not twenty years ago). Ask what paperwork you need to file, and then double-check anything they tell you with the state educational department.

Why both? The parent can break everything down into actionable, real-life tasks, and the department can give you the actual letter of the law or forms needed for compliance. Between the two, you should get what you need to move forward.

2. Choose *What* You Will Teach

Most parents launch headfirst into picking curriculum at this stage, which I believe is a step or two ahead of where they should be. Before you decide what books and software you'll use, you should know what subjects you'll cover. How do you decide? Your state may have requirements (math, reading, or physical education), and you'll want to teach the mandatory subjects above all else.

Then, work in the things they would likely learn in public school, such as history, science, or literature. Make a list of no more than six or seven classes for the year. You won't teach them all at once on day one. It's tempting to throw in everything you've ever wanted to learn as a child, but violin, advanced Mandarin, and oral interpretation of drama can all wait until you get fully adjusted. (More on choosing extracurriculars later.)

3. Decide *How* You Will Teach

Now comes what I think is the most challenging part of home-schooling. If you get it right, however, you'll save years of time, frustration, and money. I'll freely admit that it took us many trials to figure out our teaching style. As our family's needs and schedule changed, so did the way we taught. When I was home nursing a new baby with several other tiny children around, we did more open-ended learning, with fewer textbooks and more play. As the kids grew, we invested in more formal online learning opportunities, with courses taught by professors and experts in their field. We frequently adjusted our methods and expectations, as our time and financial resources fluctuated. In other words, we made do with what we had.

Part of figuring out how you'll teach comes from answering questions. I'd start by making a list and talking these over with your partner or whoever else cares for the kids:

- How many hours a day do we truly have available to teach with one-on-one instruction?
- How much are we prepared to spend on education, per child, each year?
- What value system do we want reflected in learning resources? Do we care if the approach is agnostic, faith-based, or created with a philosophical view in mind?

- How do we feel about screen time? How many hours of video learning or app-based subjects are we willing to allow?
- Do we have the time or patience to mix and match curriculum and tools? Or would we rather buy an entire program from one vendor that we trust?
- How does my child best learn? Are there learning challenges, such as speech difficulties or sensory needs, that should be addressed?
- Do we have children who can learn some subjects together?
- What teaching methods are my trusted friends and peers using? What do they like best about them? What do they say are the challenges?

Some of these questions will require you to think hard about your child—both their personality and their capabilities. If they've been in regular school for some time, you may not even know some answers. For instance, if you aren't sure how your child best learns, that's okay (and don't be afraid to ask their current or recent teacher!). Any information you have at this point will only help you make better decisions, but there will be a period of discovery with your child when you may be surprised by what they already know.

4. Sample Your Top Curriculum Choices

In your research and conversations with other parents, you'll probably hear the same curriculum brands over and over. While there are some brands that are extremely popular, they aren't the only names out there. Feel free to explore whatever programs you think fall in line with the answers to your questions in the previous step. Make a list of those that you think might work, then begin sampling.

How can you sample? Depending on the product, you can try before you buy one of these ways:

- Sign up for a free trial of software or a learning app, usually for seven to thirty days.
- Use the "Look Inside" feature on Amazon to see the contents of a book and how the text looks and reads.
- Visit the publisher's website for a textbook and take advantage of the sample pages many offer for download.
- Ask to borrow a friend's copy of a textbook or workbook.
- Check out a book or an ebook from the library to get a feel for the text.

To get an idea if a product will work, you don't necessarily need to sit your kid down and go through the motions of learning. Some books will immediately seem like a bad fit, as maybe they feature worldviews that conflict with those of your family or they use a tone that's too formal, and are therefore off-putting. Others will have great bones, but the accessories or workbooks will feel wrong. Still others may have excellent online videos but offer out-of-date texts. You're the parent, so go with your gut. In addition to having quality educational content, the product should be engaging enough to keep your child's attention.

A Word on Self-Guided Learning

One myth that many new homeschoolers bring with them is that they need to be the "teacher" for every part of their child's learning. They assume that they will stand at one end of the dining room, a whiteboard behind them, reading prompts from a giant manual while their youngster copies down notes and raises their hand.

Drop this expectation right now.

Yes, especially when the kids are younger, you will sometimes have to sit with them and coach them through topics they find challenging. You're also more than welcome to sit at the table with your child, demonstrating math facts or telling them about your time visiting a foreign country or even doing read-alouds (because you love reading aloud, and kids love listening to it).

Once a child can read independently—and sometimes long before that—there's a good amount of work they can do on their own. You'll need to plan the work and get it ready for them. You can explain new things to them and stand by them as they go through those first few worksheets on their own. You can be available for questions as they arise and check answers and administer tests. You can also take a more self-guided approach.

When a child can read on their own, you have a world of "independent learning" options available to you. These may look just like traditional textbooks, but instead of being written for a teacher to present to the student, they're written directly to the student. They assume that this text (or video, in some cases) is the instruction. It stands alone as the expert in the room. It doesn't assume you'll be standing there as the teacher.

Can these programs really work? Yes, for the right student. A self-guided learning program will have the student read or watch a certain amount each day, then answer questions or put answers in a workbook for the parent to check. Tests and quizzes are given as usual. The parent can see gaps in learning right away, and there's always an opportunity to explore further together. For the parent who has limited time or multiple students at home, self-guided learning can be a godsend.

Not only does it save all that "instruction time" you may not have much of, it gives kids something very precious: It teaches them to be responsible for their own learning, something that will come in handy when they reach college (not to mention the rest of the world!). Many of the best postsecondary classes today require mostly self-guided learning or independent study; your child will be poised to excel in this learning environment.

5. Buy Just What You Need (for Now) and Begin

Now that you think you've found the right materials or online resources for your child, you can start shopping. Go slow, buying what you need for one course at a time, if you can. This gives you a chance to try the courses in practice and makes it easier to change if you don't like what you see.

Yes, you can sometimes get some really good deals when you buy an entire year's worth of curriculum from one publisher or virtual school, but be careful. While the discount can be substantial, it's only a bargain if you use all the materials. (Those with buyer's remorse won't feel that they saved at all.) Save this type of bulk buying for when you've used a company's materials for long enough to know that you really love them. You'll have many years ahead to get the big discounts on larger curriculum packages.

Note: If there's a stereotype that fits most homeschoolers I know, it's that they love to shop for curricula. We tend to overbuy, and those shiny curriculum catalogs are like catnip to those of us who only want the best educational opportunities for our children. It's also common to experience FOMO (fear of missing out); parents may think that everyone else has upgraded to the latest edition of a book, so they must as well. If the hundreds of barely used textbooks that go on sale at sites like eBay tell you anything, it's that overbuying is a real struggle. We love to get our hands on the next promising teaching tool, but we quickly learn that it's not the magical answer we expected it to be.

If you want to avoid boxes of unused books and long hours reselling online, start small. Buy one thing at a time. Fully test each new thing so that you can be sure it's a fit. And when you find out that it's not—because even seasoned homeschoolers can misjudge how well a tool will work—forgive yourself. Homeschool materials have a particularly good resale value.

6. Adjust and Try Again. And Again.

I recommend that parents try one subject first, get acquainted with how it will work, then add a second. It may take a week or more to get to the point of adding in a second subject, and that's okay. Legally, most states want you to spend a certain number of hours teaching within a year, and you can certainly fit it all in, even by easing into it slowly. This also saves frustration for the newly home-schooling parent who's trying to balance it all.

An example might look like this:

- Week 1: Start with math. Do a few fun activities, such as learning videos or games, to break up the down-time. Go on a field trip or create a craft on Friday.

- Week 2: Add language arts to the mix. Check in with your child to see that they're progressing at both. Don't hesitate to pull back if it feels over-whelming.

- Week 3: Work up to three subjects now, making sure you're saving time for those other fun activities that were done in week 1. Add in twenty to thirty minutes of quiet reading time each day.

- Week 4: By now, you could have four subjects, a full plate for most kids. If you're wondering how you'll get seven mandatory fifth-grade subjects this way, remember you can break up work by semesters. First semester might have a science course; second might include geography.

If at any point you experience extreme frustration from your child, stop and adjust. This doesn't mean you let them have their way, but really listen to their concerns. It may be that one simple fix to their schedule or programming could make a big difference to them. (Math in the morning may be too stressful; moving it to the afternoon, after a snack and some downtime, could be the answer.)

Give yourself more than four weeks to find your groove. For some of our kids, it took years. If they're moving ahead, they're learning. Allow adequate time for breaks. (More on scheduling in Chapter 5.)

Note: If your child was removed from the public or private school system, they may be having more trouble than you expected. This is normal. See page 208 for how to meet this challenge head-on. (It's actually not a bad problem to have.)

MORE CURRICULUM SHOPPING TIPS

For the newbie homeschooler, nothing is more daunting than picking a curriculum. I understand the stress. Not only can picking the wrong thing be expensive but it feels like a waste of time to spend too long on a set of books or online courses that don't do anything for your child.

Lynnae McCoy, who has had her kids in public, private, and homeschool over the years, shares this thoughtful advice about the importance of picking the right curriculum (or rather why it's not as important as we think):

"You're in charge of the curriculum, not the other way around," she says. "The first year of homeschooling is like the first year of parenting: you learn as you go. If something isn't working, it's okay to modify it to fit your needs. Just because the curriculum says you need to take a nature walk on Wednesdays doesn't mean it's set in stone. Take a walk on Fridays. Or don't take a walk. Explore nature in your backyard. If your child is frustrated because there's too much writing in the curriculum, do some of the work orally. The huge benefit to homeschooling is the ability to encourage kids to love the learning process. If you teach kids to love learning, they'll be miles ahead of where they would be if you check all the boxes but they hate learning."

Lynnae approaches learning the way I do, and like so many other homeschoolers do. She encourages parents to enjoy the process and not be afraid to learn with their kids. You can discover together, read together, and research all the new facts and topics that you'll be experiencing. These priceless moments are what make homeschooling unique. It truly can't be replicated anywhere else.

Chapter 3

HOMESCHOOL LEGALITIES AND REQUIREMENTS

The next question I usually get after someone asks "How do I homeschool?" is "But how about homeschooling in my state?" While it's now legal to homeschool in all fifty states, the lengths you must go to comply will vary.

I'm not going to lay out all the requirements for homeschooling in each state because, while it doesn't happen very often, they do change. These changes may be very minor clarifications in the law, but they can make a difference in how you approach your home education goals. It's also very hard to summarize the rules for each state because it really is the detail that gets you. Some states are very picky about signing a form correctly or providing the right kind of documentation. Entire chapters could be written on just how to do it well in each state.

So, I'll lay out your first steps to homeschooling legally in your state.

1. CHECK WITH YOUR STATE

That may sound obvious, but it's not. Usually, when I speak to someone who's homeschooling for the first time, I find that they've hopped on Facebook or asked their friends how to fill out paperwork. You can do this, but I prefer to check the letter of the law. Those laws are found, most likely, with your state Department of Education. Do an internet search for your state's name and "Department of Education." Add in "homeschool" if you like. You'll probably get the page that has filing rules and frequently asked questions for you to peruse.

What if your state doesn't have a law? I'm quite sure it does, but you may live in a state that doesn't have filing or notification requirements. Texas and Missouri are two such states (at the time of this writing) that don't require you to fill out forms and let the government know what you'll be doing or whom you'll be teaching. Your state may also call homeschooling by another term; in Nebraska, homeschools are called "exempt schools."

Don't confuse not having to notify the state of your decision with not having to follow any rules. You'll still have some standards to set. These might include a set number of instructional hours, classes taught, or ages taught.

2. VISIT WITH OTHER HOMESCHOOLERS

The homeschool community can be very helpful when trying to be compliant with the law. That's because the law isn't really written for people to easily understand, and it may take some friendly talks over coffee with your peers to help you get on board. Ask them to show you examples of their documentation, such as portfolios. They can help you find a testing solution, if assessments are required. They may also know the best time to contact the Department of Education with questions, and how long to wait before following up.

3. CONSIDER AN ADVOCACY GROUP

It's much easier to go down a road that's already been paved for you, and that's why I suggest any homeschooler check out what the Home School Legal Defense Association (HSLDA) has to offer. While this organization was founded and run by Christians, it's open to anyone, regardless of personal beliefs or political leanings. As long as you want to homeschool and support the freedom for parents to choose the educational direction for their child, you'll be a good fit for the organization. They count over ninety-five thousand member families and supporters.

There's some free advice on the site that you can access without becoming a member. This includes the groups page, which has network listings by state, plus some national resources that parents in any state can access. (Some of these cost money to join, but having an active membership in the HSLDA can sometimes get you discounts on these groups and other memberships.)

They also have a very thorough set of articles and guides, by state, on how to homeschool your child legally. For Nebraska, where I live, they have an overview of the laws and the actions parents must take in the first year—and every year after—to stay compliant. They even include forms for withdrawing your child from school and for interacting with the district. These forms are available only to members, but the rest of the information is available to anyone.

Additional resources for HSLDA members include planners, portfolio recommendations, organization sheets, and anything else you'd need to show a government official in the course of homeschooling. While home visits and calls from the school district aren't common, HSLDA and its team aim to make sure you're equipped to handle them in case they occur.

4. KNOW YOUR TOOLS

States may require you to keep a number of documents in order to prove, if asked, that you're actually homeschooling. Other states require that these documents be turned in or assessed regularly. They include:

Attendance Sheet

This shows which days you homeschool, including the number of hours each day (if required). Some states need a detailed breakdown of this time, while others may be satisfied with a simple checkmark next to a date on a calendar. Your homeschool planner, if you buy one premade, most likely has a section for attendance.

Grades and Assessments

Do you track assignments, quizzes, and tests? You might need to. Some states don't care if you keep grades; others do, to show that your child is progressing. Still others may require you to use standardized testing services from a list of preapproved vendors annually, or every four years, as a way of documenting that your child is making progress.

Portfolio

What the heck is a portfolio? For different parents and states, it can mean different things. Examples of portfolios that may work for your state include three-ring binders with all major test results, writing samples, photos of any crafts, and documentation of field trips, books read, or activities enrolled in. You may also want to include some photo album pages to store larger sheets of artwork. Check your state's requirements for portfolio details, but this is definitely one area where seeing what other parents do is very helpful. Portfolios can be a useful tool even if they aren't mandatory. Having a nice record of your child's accomplishments can help motivate you, and you'll love looking back on it as they grow.

How to Store Your Records

If you're living under a pile of papers, books, toys, and laundry, you're probably a typical parent just trying to get through the day. Now that you've added homeschooling to the list, it may feel overwhelming.

So, what can you do to keep all your homeschool stuff safe and sorted? I would think about your organizational personality and go from there. While there are some shiny products and services on the market that promise to simplify homeschool record-keeping, they all require you to enter data and keep everything updated. If you don't like the format, find it technologically confusing, or can't access it regularly, you won't use it—and that defeats the purpose.

Here are some of the options parents are using today to keep their homeschool stuff together (in addition to the three-ring binder portfolio mentioned above). Which one matches your current style?

File Folders

Choose between expandable files or simple manila style. Keep them someplace safe from fire or flood, such as a locked protective box or small filing cabinet. Be sure to keep them sorted as you put new files in, or it can become very messy and confusing for anyone hoping to find one particular document later.

Paper Homeschool Planners

I go over planning a bit more in Chapter 5, but you can most definitely make your planner work double duty as a record of your schooling. I save calendars and planners every year, even though my state doesn't require super-detailed notes. It's fun to look back and see what we worked on each year.

Digital Planners and Tools

Not a fan of paper clutter in your home? Worried you'll spill coffee on those precious records—or lose them altogether? Then digital, cloud-based tools may be for you. There are dozens to choose from, and some are made with homeschoolers specifically in mind. The more detailed ones require a monthly or annual membership, which means you have to keep paying to access your files. If you can stay diligent about updating your information frequently, however, this is a good bet for managing multiple children and a busy schedule.

Cloud Storage Services

Many online providers, like Google Drive, give you some storage for free. You can create your own documents, spreadsheets, and scans of artwork and upload to the cloud for safekeeping. You might also want to snap photos of your files to store on your phone's storage service (such as Apple iCloud). Remember to back up your stuff often.

THE BOTTOM LINE ON STAYING LEGAL

With so many differences in the way states handle homeschooling, it's impossible to give even general guidelines on following the law. But definitely keep the following in mind if you're interested in homeschooling:

1. **Research Ahead of Time (if Possible).** Of course, you won't always have a lot of notice if you need to pull your kid from school. But if you do, start digging into the rules for your state and lay the groundwork. Find out what paperwork is required, and when.

2. **File.** If your state requires it, do all the paperwork. Don't do it partially or late. Get it done.

3. **Keep Records.** Know what you need and how long to keep it. When in doubt, keep more than you need and scan things to save space with digital copies. Document the things your state requires.

4. **Stay on Task.** Do you need to test? Are you required to keep a portfolio? Are you subject to the oversight of a homeschool evaluator? Know what you need to do and when throughout the year. Don't wait to be told that you've forgotten something.

5. **Be Informed.** Even if you've never watched a legislative proceeding in your life, now's the time to at least know what's going on with education in your state. Often homeschoolers can positively influ-

ence lawmakers to keep home education legal and free of undue burdens on the families that do it. By knowing about any educational policies coming up in your state, you can take action, if needed, to protect your right to lead your child's education. The HSLDA email newsletters are a fantastic source of information on things happening at the state and federal level that affect all students, particularly home-educated children.

WHY CUSTODY AGREEMENTS MATTER

Married couples don't always agree on whether homeschool is the right move for their kids. So it should come as no surprise that homeschooling is a hot-button issue for divorcing or already divorced parents. If one wants to homeschool and the other doesn't, it can be a problem—even if the parent who wants to homeschool has physical custody.

I can't give legal advice on how to handle these situations, but you should know that most states require the permission of both parents to allow homeschooling. Even in those states where you don't have to notify the authorities or file as a homeschooler, a parent who disapproves of homeschooling can bring it up as a custody issue. If possible, work with your legal team and former spouse or partner to get everyone on board. Beyond legalities, homeschooling works best for kids when both parents value the opportunities it provides.

If things do get difficult, make sure educational rights are addressed in the custody paperwork. Even uncontested divorces should specifically lay out who makes the final call on education matters, and homeschooling should be left on the table as an option for that parent.

WHAT HAPPENS IF YOU FACE LEGAL PROBLEMS?

I hope you never get a knock on your door from authorities asking about homeschooling. If you've done your research and followed through on the rules, it's highly unlikely. But things happen, and that's why having a legal advocacy group is useful. Contacting your personal attorney or reaching out to your HSLDA contact is advised in any situation in which someone is threatening legal, criminal, or civil action against you in the course of educating your children.

{ *Chapter 4* }

TOOLS OF THE TRADE

What if you learned that you had to start homeschooling tomorrow, and that you had twenty-four hours to gather everything you needed to do it successfully? What would be on your list? How much of it would you already have in your home?

Yes, you'll need things like paper, pens, and books. A computer would be nice. But with so many companies trying to get your homeschool dollar, how can you know what's absolutely necessary, and what's just fluff? This chapter includes the very basics of what to buy—in addition to your curriculum and books. The amazing part is that you likely have many of these things in your home already. The rest can be introduced as you can afford them (thanks to the tips in Chapter 7).

WRITING UTENSILS

When you think of writing tools, does the famous yellow no. 2 pencil spring to mind? Today's kids have so many more writing tools to choose from, and I'm thankful for that. Depending on your homeschool style and the needs of your kid, you may find that the no. 2 pencil shows up only for formal tests, like the ACT or CLT (Classic Learning Test, an alternative to traditional tests that's slowly growing in popularity).

So what should you use? I'm a fan of the pen, even for math and especially for creative writing, cursive lessons, and note-taking. The benefits of pens haven't been largely talked about, but Andrew Pudewa, the founder and director of the Institute for Excellence in Writing (IEW), shares some ideas about why kids are attracted to using a pen for schoolwork, and why you may want to make the switch.

In a 2001 IEW newsletter article, Pudewa mentions these as some of the perks of pens:[1]

- They limit handwriting fatigue, since you don't have to press down as hard to get clear, dark lines.
- They offer a smooth, consistent writing experience, unlike pencils, which dull over time.
- They reduce some of the distractions that come from worrying about lead breakage and sharpening—leaving kids to focus on their learning.

Not only do they work really well for kids with sensory processing issues, they break kids of the habit of always erasing their mistakes. (I'm not a fan of erasing mistakes, since it doesn't let you see how they got to a correct answer, and it often takes longer to erase a sentence than to cross it out and rewrite a new one!) As children grow, they may become preoccupied with always writing down answers right the first time. Pens encourage them to see learning as a process where the first time isn't always correct, and this opens the door to learning some of the proofreading marks that will be helpful later on in grammar and composition classes.

Finally, I know a lot of parents who want their kids to mark their consumable, one-time-use workbooks in pencil. Then the parent erases them so they can be used again. If the only reason you're using pencils in your homeschool is to save money on the cost of a workbook, I'd encourage you to consider the benefits of pens and see if they may offer better overall value to your child's development.

(For help on how to save money with consumable workbooks, see Chapter 7. It's always advisable to follow the copyright guidelines for any homeschool materials to see if copying them is an option.)

Whether you go with pens or pencils, small hands may require some help to master proper pencil grip. I can't say enough good things about The Pencil Grip, Inc., which offers a variety of grip options for kids of all ages, stages, and needs.

ADDITIONAL SCHOOL SUPPLIES

I'll never forget the look on a cashier's face when I loaded up the school supplies for my kids, and she asked, "What school makes you buy all that?" I explained that we were a homeschooling family, and big one at that. She didn't seem to understand why homeschoolers needed the same scissors, glue, notebooks, and markers that other classrooms needed. While we have some flexibility in what we buy—and how we use it—a good set of supplies is always essential.

I buy all our school supplies at the beginning of the school year, just a week or so before the public and private schools put out their supply lists. This gives us the best selection, since everyone is still waiting to see how many crayons they'll need. We also get the same great deals everyone else gets. I can't get enough twenty-five-cent wide-ruled notebooks!

Things you want to be sure to stock up on include:

- washable-ink markers
- crayons
- rulers
- protractors for upper grades
- wide-ruled or college-ruled notebooks (depending on age)
- graphic notebooks (for science lab reports)
- pencil sharpeners
- three-hole punch

- stapler and staples
- paper clips and binder clips
- folders (style depends on use)
- binders for storing folders and projects

Nice-to-haves that I enjoy (but that aren't absolutely essential) include:

- laminator and laminating sheets
- whiteboard
- dry erase markers

I wait until these go on deep sale online. Don't rush out unless you absolutely know you need them.

If you have art lessons on your agenda, see what specialty items you might need. Art requirements are pretty specific, especially for pencils, which vary in softness. You may need a special kneaded eraser, graphite stick, and various paper surfaces for a simple beginner's sketching course. Paint or modeling classes will require even more!

ORGANIZATIONAL TOOLS

You can spend a lot here, and I recommend families keep it simple until they fully understand their needs. A shoebox or laundry basket can work until you figure out how your family's day will look and how people and activities flow through the home. Then you can move to caddies for each kid, although I suggest they be something your children can take with them to whatever corner of the room they want to work in. This helps younger kids stay out of the older kids' expensive art markers, and it helps everyone learn how to be accountable for their own supplies. Plastic tubs aren't a replacement for learning good habits.

Try as you may, of course, stuff will go missing. (Did you think that homeschooling was going to be a cure for your child who's always losing his notebook?) It can be tempting to jump in and help your child find his missing items, especially when you have a schedule to keep and he's holding himself up. If you do this too often, however, you'll teach your kid that you'll always be there to clean up after him. Homeschool parents have to try harder to not "helicopter." You can set them up with the right tools, but don't enable bad behavior. Give them a free pass now and again, but if they miss class because they don't have what they need, they have to find their things and make it up on the weekend.

TECH TOOLS

Tech is a large category of consumer products, and with more and more homeschooling happening with software and online courses, it makes sense that more tech would be involved. The following items are all things we use in our homeschool, but don't think that you need to run out and buy everything on the list just for the learning mission. You probably have many of these things in your home already, and this checklist can help you determine if what you own will meet the demands of the home learner. If it doesn't, it isn't permission to break the budget; just keep these guidelines in mind for when you do upgrade. Shopping for a new printer, for example, is much easier when you know how you'll use it and what features it should offer.

Computer or Laptop

Computers may be the most expensive purchase you make for your homeschool, and even if your kids' courses are 90 percent offline, you'll use a computer for keeping records, printing worksheets, research, and typing classes. If you already have something in the home, use that. If you do need to shop, such as with multiple kids taking online courses, or you don't want your school kids using your business laptop, shop early for the best price and selection.

How do you know if a laptop or desktop computer is for you? Ask yourself these questions before you buy:

- Do you have a dedicated workspace accessible to everyone? If so, you can choose a laptop or desktop.

- Are you limited by budget? Laptops are more expensive than desktops with the same processing, graphic, memory, and storage capacities.

- Do you need to move from room to room or "roadschool?" A laptop is the way to go.

- Are you unable to decide between a tablet or computer? Consider a convertible laptop that features a touch screen and folds up from laptop mode to tablet mode. These laptops can also work with digital pens for drawing or note-taking.

- Do you hate shopping and just want to buy everything in one box? A laptop should suffice, but you can also go with an all-in-one desktop with the computer tower built into the monitor. These computers come with everything at purchase, so you can plug and play within minutes.

- Are you going to use your school computer for gaming? Even if you're putting your foot down about using the school computer for entertainment, many of the best desktops have the power to play some pretty exciting and resource-intensive games. If gaming is even a slight possibility—and more educational games are being made all the time—consider investing in a computer that can handle it now.

A Note on Chromebooks and Other Pared-Down Laptops

School systems have been incorporating more laptops into the classroom, so you may already have experience using Chromebooks,

Streams, and other lower-priced laptops. They're affordable, work well with existing public school programs, and are easy for even younger kids to carry (not to mention, they're incredibly durable).

Are these school picks right for your homeschool? On the surface, they appear like any other laptop, but it's what's inside that counts. Many of these laptops feature very low memory and storage, as they assume you'll be using them in conjunction with web-based tools and cloud storage services. The processor and graphics aren't always up to the demands of more computing-intensive applications, such as design, editing, and gaming software. Some homeschoolers have reported that the browsers installed aren't compatible with their live learning courses. While they can be a blessing to the budget, don't assume that a computer made for institutional or school use is going to cut it for full-time learning in your home. Invest in the features you need to be successful.

When a Tablet May Suffice

Can you get away with using an iPad, Kindle, or Android-based tablet? It depends on what you use it for. For educational apps that you download from the Apple Store, for example, an iPad is a must. Beyond that use, however, you may find it lacking.

Not all tablets are compatible with all web-based learning programs; others lack the storage and processing to handle big creative tasks. Kindle Fire tablets only work with Amazon-based apps, and not all educational service providers have made the leap to this technology. Tablets are good for games, apps, video conferencing, and reading ebooks, but you shouldn't expect them to stand in for a computer.

CD Player or DVD Player

Do people still listen to CDs? In the homeschool world, they do. While publishers are making the switch to providing course materials via online streaming services and digital downloads, some of the best products are still available only on disc. If you're like most families and don't have a CD player handy, look at how you can use an existing gaming system or computer to play essential tracks.

DVDs are still the choice for some lesson providers as well. We got around this by investing in an affordable external CD/DVD-ROM drive that can plug into our laptop with a USB cable. It can be shared between devices. Another favorite gadget for homeschool families is an e-reader, like a Kindle or a Nook. Your child may need to read digital versions of books in their homeschool, so having a family e-reader may be a good investment (after all, you can read on it, too!). In addition to reading all those free classics that Amazon and Google have made available for download, you can load them up with apps.

Full disclosure: I'm a huge fan of the Kindle Fire. It's saved me on many business trips with my toddler on my lap for a four-hour delayed flight. It's also incredibly tempting to use it more than you should, so create boundaries for your child around how long they can play. The Kindle Fire has Amazon Kids and Amazon Kids+ services that, for just a few dollars a month, give your kids access to an entire library of popular books, games, and videos from Amazon Prime. The best part is the parental controls, which allow you to cap the child's time, limit what games or books they access, and even "assign" a set number of minutes by activity. (Making your child read an assigned ebook for twenty minutes before they play the latest LEGO app has never been easier!)

Shared TV and a Casting Device

Have you ever watched multiple kids try to crowd around a computer monitor or laptop screen for a shared gaming or movie experience? Avoid this same frustration when teaching video classes to more than one student by streaming content from your PC or laptop to your family's television. The Google Chromecast is one way to get this done, and it works with your computer's Chrome browser to share anything from your computer to the larger television. This way everyone can spread out and get comfy while they learn!

Headphones

What's worse than hearing the whistles and bells from a child playing a video game in close proximity to you? I personally cannot deal with so much noise, and I request that my kids use headphones when gaming, watching videos, or using educational apps. In our small home, this is one way to maintain my calm, but it's also helpful when kids are using live video courses, as it helps cut down on the background noise coming from our house. And, of course, it's the polite thing to do for everyone else on the video call.

If you're concerned about hearing loss, which is a legitimate danger from wearing headphones often (and at high levels), invest in a set that's made specifically for kids and meets guidelines for safe decibel levels. This type of equipment can't exceed levels deemed harmful for children, no matter how high they try turning up the volume on their device. While not a substitute for monitoring your child's headphone use and teaching them about safety, they can help support healthy listening practices. They also fit better on smaller children's heads.

Printer

If there's one tool that you don't skimp on, please, let it be the printer. I see too many parents buy the absolute cheapest printer they can, and they pay for it with pricey ink and an inability to do all the cool things printers can do these days. At a minimum, your printer must have print, scan, and copy functions (fax is often unnecessary). You'll use this to print out worksheets, copy consumables (if allowed by the company's usage agreement), scan children's artwork, and keep your records together.

The newer printers are completely wireless, practically set themselves up, and can even send for a new shipment of ink automatically. If you invest in a nice enough printer, you need only one for the whole house, since it can connect to your home wireless network and receive print jobs from any connected device, such as a mobile phone or tablet.

High-Speed Internet

Here's the thing about high-speed internet: It's getting faster all the time, but not everyone has it. If you live in a rural area, like me, you probably drool when you see families bragging about their 1,000 Mbps (or more) Google Fiber speeds. These speeds are awesome, and someday maybe we'll get them. In the meantime, you should know that most online course programs and streaming resources require at least 1–2 Mbps download speeds and 1Mbps for upload. If you want to do live classes, you'll want to double that.

Keep in mind that these speeds are for one person using the internet. If you have several kids gaming or doing online courses at once, you'll need that speed for each. If your speeds are still too slow, or you can't access them during peak periods of the day, consider an asynchronous (offline) learning resource. Always inquire with any company about the internet speed requirements for their resources before purchasing. You don't want to waste your money on a course or tool that you can't get to load when you need it.

In a pinch, you can use phone data plans, mobile hot spots, or tethering options. If you need to do this often, however, it may cost you more in data than it's worth. Since you pick the curriculum, be realistic about your internet needs, and don't settle on any program that requires you to dig into your phone's data plan regularly.

Security Software or Monitoring Apps

Whether you homeschool or not, it's always a good idea to have security software on your computers and devices. In addition to a firewall, I recommend an antivirus and anti-malware program that can run on its own and is frequently updated against the newest threats. This will help you avoid corrupted devices, ransomware, and hacks to your personal information.

Additionally, look into what kind of family-friendly protections you can put on your computer. These aren't a substitute for having frequent conversations with your kids about what they're looking at online, but they can be an additional safeguard, especially for younger kids. It's easy to mistype a bad word into Google or click an external link to a YouTube video you wouldn't want them watching. Every safeguard you can implement matters.

The major software developers, such as Symantec (Norton) and McAfee, are a good place to start. You can also try some independent developers, but check online to see their reputation before you install anything on your computer. You might also want to use a router-based solution to monitor kids' time online, restrict access to sites or games that may distract them from schoolwork, and prevent the downloading of documents or programs without your permission. Not only will you be protecting your devices from bugs and viruses, it's a neighborly thing to do in a time when kids are online with others in live classroom situations. Some live courses may even require you to have precautions installed to keep it safe for everyone in the session.

Most threats to your children won't come in the form of pop-ups, accidental adult videos, or sketchy game downloads. In fact, a Center for Cyber Safety and Education study reported the following eye-opening statistics about kids in grades four through eight:[2]

- 21 percent of kids visit sites where they can talk to strangers
- 40 percent of kids chatted with a stranger online
- 11 percent of the kids who connected with a stranger later met a stranger in real life

Surprisingly, 87 percent of kids are taught about the dangers of the internet, but 29 percent of them admit to using the Web in ways they shouldn't. This shows us that it's not enough to talk to kids about the internet once or twice. We must always be in conversation, actively checking on them to see that they're making good decisions.

As more and more of homeschool moves online, there will be more opportunities for kids to have extra browser tabs or chat apps open while they "do their school." Don't be shy about holding them accountable. Good parents don't apologize for putting their kids' safety first.

A Word on Sharing Resources

Should your family use one computer for work and school? As a business owner who writes for many companies in a variety of industries, I'm often fighting with my kids for bandwidth, access to the printer, and a quiet space in the home. But I don't share my computer with my kids. My computer is a work computer, paid for with my work money, and taken as a deduction on my tax returns. Not only is this separation necessary to establish boundaries in my work and home life (and to be IRS-compliant), I deal with many confidential documents and logins in the course of my workday. The thought of my six-year-old playing *Minecraft* with the same computer I use to edit a Fortune 500 company's Google Doc terrifies me. Keep it separate.

(If the budget makes this hard, consider a cheap tablet for the kids to use for a short time. It's not worth jeopardizing your career or business to let your kid use learning apps.)

{ *Chapter 5* }

SAMPLE SCHEDULES
AND PROPER PLANNING

Some people are natural-born schedulers. They keep meticulous records of what they want to do each day, and even better records of how they fared in meeting those goals.

I am not one of those people.

No matter where you fall on the organizational spectrum, you may be surprised to learn that there are some very general rules on how long it takes to homeschool. Because kids are human, and humans have limits, you can schedule as much as you want in a day, but they will only be able to sit, absorb, and review for so much of it.

So, how long is too long? What can we expect from a kinder-gartner compared to a high schooler? When asking dozens of parents (and even a few experts) their opinions on the appropriate length of time to learn each day, I found the answers to be very close—no matter the method or style of homeschooling.

Classical homeschoolers, unschoolers, and those with access to private tutors all agree that there are caps on a kid's energy and concentration. Here some of the best samples I got when inquiring:

KHAN ACADEMY

This reputable online learning provider came up with their own sample schedules when the coronavirus pandemic caused many parents to bring schooling home for the first time in 2020. "What should I have my kids do?" many asked. Not only did Khan continue to provide their courses for free, they set age-level guidance for how long kids should learn in a day. Based on their sample schedules, they recommend:[1]

- **Preschool, Kindergarten, 1st grade and 2nd grade:** 1 hour, 40 minutes
- **Grades 3–5:** 3 hours, 20 minutes
- **Grades 6–9:** 4 hours, 20 minutes
- **Grades 10–12:** 4 hours, 20 minutes

Khan set up schedules that filled an entire day, but the times listed above are the total time during the day when kids would be formally learning, such as completing an online math course, practicing penmanship, or reading from books. Free time, such as playing outside, snacking, listening to podcasts, or hanging out with family members, is not included in my total above, although my opinion is that these activities are just as valuable (if not more so) in creating well-rounded, educated kids.

How do Khan Academy's recommendations stack up against actual homeschool parent experiences? Here are a few schedules from real families. See how they compare:

LYNNAE McCOY (HOMESCHOOLS A TEN-YEAR-OLD):

"We probably school for three and a half to four hours a day on a long day. Some days are shorter, but we incorporate learning into everyday life, too. We do Bible and maybe one other reading at breakfast. After we get ready for the day, we move on to social science, science, language arts, and anything else I need to be directly involved in. We finish the day with math and independent reading, which are things my daughter can do mostly on her own."

MELISSA BATAI:

"The girls are now in fifth and sixth grade, and we homeschool roughly four hours a day. We homeschool year-round, typically only taking off two to four weeks a year, so we don't have to do as much every day as a family that wants the entire summer off."

Melissa uses a more formalized schedule approach, and she shares what it looks like in a typical day in her home:

8:00–8:30	Literature read-alouds
8:30–9:00	Religion
9:00–9:30	Break
9:30–10:30	Science, Writing, and/or Japanese
10:30–11:30	Break
11:30–12:00	Lunch
12:00–2:00	Time with tutor for special-needs learning program
2:00–2:30	Math

Even with this more formalized schedule, Melissa doesn't spend more than four hours or so with formal learning. She makes a point to squeeze in some extra enrichment time, such as bedtime reading, when she can. She also shares her thoughts on mistakes she sees with some homeschoolers:

"I've seen some new homeschoolers lament that the curriculum is taking them six to eight hours to get through with their kids. In my opinion, that's just too long. Maybe high school might take that long, but anything eighth grade and below should definitely take less than six hours. Don't let the curriculum dictate what you do. You decide how much schooling your kids can take in a day."

JOANNA COMPTON:

"Grades nine and ten were done in about four hours a day. We covered most of our core subjects in these two years, including completing foreign language credits, PE, and fine arts. Grades eleven and twelve were about two to three hours a day, as they were doing more 'delight' learning, such as guitar, ukulele, and theater, as well as electives—things they were interested in."

This mother sets a limit of three hours for her elementary-level students, with kids in kindergarten through second grade doing less. As the kids age, she gradually increases formal learning time, with middle schoolers getting between three and four hours a day, and high schoolers getting more.

• • •

As you can see from these replies, each of our parents has their own unique approach to how they fit homeschooling into the day. No matter how formal the learning, however, they seem to all agree that there is a distinct limit to how long they can expect kids to learn. When the goal is joyful learning and a love for things like reading, math, or science, sometimes less is more.

One mother, someone with grown children and years of homeschool experience, may have said it best. Listen to what Erin Manning has to say about the learning limits and expectations she set for her kids, and why it's important to not push too much formalized teaching into a day.

"This is something I always try to share with new homeschooling moms, because I think the idea of the long school day of six or more hours plus homework is so ingrained that we forget how much of that time is not used for education—and how much of it gets spent repeating something a child may already understand, because half of his or her classmates haven't grasped the concept yet," she says.

Erin's ideal schedule looks like this:

Kindergarten students should have about forty-five minutes of actual instruction in a day, including letters, numbers, and a parent reading aloud. The other things that happen in kindergarten, such as arts and crafts, exercise, naps, snacks, meals, and playtime, will happen naturally over the course of the day.

First-, second-, and third-grade students should expect between ninety minutes and two hours on most days. This will not include time spent reading for fun, which should be encouraged early on. It will include reading assignments, writing (including short reports or essays), simple math and science, simple history, and so on.

Fourth- and fifth-grade students should experience an increase to two to three hours daily of schoolwork. There will be some longer written reports and more tests; math and science will require more time. This is a good time to introduce the kind of textbooks they will encounter as they get older, the sort that include lists of questions along with charts, graphs, or other interactives.

Sixth-, seventh-, and eighth-grade students can move up to the four-hour-mark maximum, as all the subjects and assignments become more complicated, and testing is more frequent.

High school students will vary, depending on grade, type of program, and student ability. This age group should take between four and six hours a day, but the flexibility of homeschooling permits the student to arrange his or her day in a way that makes sense. You can also try a college-style block schedule, such as three subjects on Monday-Wednesday-Friday and two or three more on Tuesday-Thursday. This allows students to concentrate on each subject for a longer time in pursuit of mastery.

Erin also reminds us of the unique benefit of this type of scheduling, which is that you don't have to train your kindergartner to sit in a classroom for six hours (as they quite naturally may not want to do) just because that's what may eventually be expected in high school or college. In fact, many homeschooled high schoolers experience more free time for hobbies and personal pursuits than their public- or private-schooled peers, because their four-to-six-hour school day includes all the worksheets, papers, and other extras we traditionally consider homework. Homeschoolers do the work during their school day because they can. This can also help avert the exhaustion that's so epidemic among today's high schoolers, for whom the day often starts at seven thirty and stretches until sunset, when you include sports and other extracurriculars.

PLANNING

One night a week, usually Sunday, I sit down with all the teacher manuals or lesson plans or other materials that tell me what my kids will be learning next. Based on the pace they've been keeping, I figure out how far along in their studies they can get in the week coming up. I take into account holidays and birthday parties. I try to remember any appointments or tasks that can take too much out of a day. I also look at my work schedule so that I don't plan many days of hands-on science experiments for the same days I'm expected to turn in a big writing project.

For each child, I print out a weekly task sheet. On these I put what they are to do in every subject. Some of my kids only need to be told to "complete math lessons 1–4." I know they'll get it done in between chores, playing games with their brothers, and their other schoolwork.

Other children, however, need to have their week planned out very deliberately. (These children are not always the older ones; personality plays a more important role in how they work than maturity.) They may get daily prompts, such as "Monday: Watch videos for math lesson 1 and do 3 review worksheets." With these children, I can check in at the end of the day and ask how their work went. If they didn't get to what they needed, I can step in and enforce the plan before they get too far off the weekly goal.

I make two copies of these sheets, so the child and I each have one. (Kids tend to lose things, and it's good to keep a backup.) If a spouse, grandparent, or other helper assists with homeschool accountability, make one for them, too.

As they get work done, they can check off the tasks from their weekly plan. Kids who finish early get more fun time over the weekend. Kids who don't get work done may have to read for British literature class while the rest of us watch a movie.

More than a Homeschool Tool

Homeschool planners are also capturing the household management market. Publishers assume that you're probably like most parents, juggling an increasing number of tasks. They want to give homeschoolers one planner to rule them all, and so you'll often see these sections in planners, too:

- meal planning
- chore lists
- appointment notes, such as doctor visits and vaccination due dates

Do you need all these extras? Some people do. If you already use a planner for household management, it makes sense to consider an all-in-one for homeschooling and household planning. The only real drawback I see to these is that you may not use many of the sections, forcing you to buy some worthless pages; you may also find the task of filling everything out and documenting your life exhausting. I know I do!

Again, your personality will help you decide. In the meantime, a weekly planner can keep you on task as you work to meet your larger educational goals.

Your First-Year Homeschool Plan

It's common for new homeschoolers to get very excited about their first year. No matter the reason you chose to homeschool, it's a new beginning, a chance to really explore everything under the sun in education, art, music, STEM, and more. In addition to overbuying homeschool materials, which we covered in Chapter 2, it's tempting to overschedule and overplan from the very first day.

You have that big, beautiful, blank planner in front of you. Why not fill it all in? Well, in my experience, there are some dangers in plotting out and inking in every day of the next school year.

First, things go awry. I know this, and if you're honest with yourself, you know this before you even begin. Whether your whole family gets the flu and skips school for two weeks or you ditch your original math program halfway through the year for something else, that plan you made is useless the minute you get off track.

Life changes. Your homeschool plans should change with it.

If you have everything planned out for a year in advance, in ink, in a paper planner, it can become demoralizing to see all that work go down the tubes. Instead, try penciling in a basic outline of your school year, or consider "milestones." These milestones are easy to move and change when life happens, and they are certainly less tedious to erase than 255 days of detailed lesson planning.

HOW TO SET HOMESCHOOL MILESTONES

The best way to set any goals in education is to work backward, and we'll talk about this more in the high school–specific grade guidance in Chapter 13. Here's an example of how to set a milestone for a math curriculum:

1. Go through the math index, table of contents, or lesson plan. Not all math books and products come with a plan laid out for you. It's enough to see the number of lessons, what's covered, and how long each lesson should take, however. In this example, let's say that fourth-grade math has thirty lessons, each expected to take place over a week.

2. If your homeschool starts on September 1, why wouldn't you just plan out a lesson a week for thirty

weeks and set a goal to be done by around March 30? Because of life, holiday breaks, family gatherings, and interruptions we can't always plan for. Instead, go through your calendar for the year and mark off any days you know you won't be doing school. Add in two extra weeks for unexpected happenings, and throw in one more for good measure. Now you have some wiggle room.

3. With a new finish date of May 15 or so, you're ready to create milestones. The simplest way to do this is to divide the thirty lessons into four quarters, with 7.5 lessons per quarter. I don't love uneven numbers, so I might divide into five "quarters" instead. This gives me six lessons per smaller "quarter," which I can set against my calendar of September 1 through May 15 to see how much I need to cover to stay on track.

   Put your milestones on your planner or larger family calendar. If you feel that you're getting behind, it's much easier to get back on track by working harder toward a milestone. If you fail by a little bit, you can work to make up for it during the next milestone. It's certainly much easier to course correct for a smaller milestone than to look ahead to an entire year and feel hopeless about meeting annual goals.

   My milestones would be:

Milestone 1
(by October 19):   Finish Lesson 6

Milestone 2
(by December 7):   Finish Lesson 12

Milestone 3
(by January 25):   Finish Lesson 18

Milestone 4
(by March 15):   Finish Lesson 24

Milestone 5
(by May 3):   Finish Lesson 30—ending early to give you even more flexibility!

WHAT HAPPENS IF YOU DON'T FINISH?

I'm going to fill you in on a little secret that's quickly become public knowledge, especially among educators and homeschoolers: It's okay if you don't finish.

Do you remember being in school? Do you remember getting to the very last unit, chapter, or page in your science or math book? How about history?

Neither do I.

I wondered if this was just my experience, or even a sign of something going on at my school. When talking to educator friends and those who know about curriculum planning, many of them have the same shared knowledge. It's common to not finish a textbook or curriculum option. So, does this mean that you have to?

There are two schools of thought on this. Some homeschoolers insist that just because public schools don't expect to finish, we shouldn't hold ourselves to the same standard. Others are understanding of the time crunch and insist that there are other ways to make up the work (or even go around it).

My approach acknowledges that we should provide the best education possible for our children, but that finishing the textbook isn't the only way to meet that aim. Here are some questions that will help you evaluate your options:

1. What Does Your Textbook Cover? Is It All New Material?

If your choice of curriculum truly introduces only new material in a school year, and that material must be learned to progress to the next level or grade in that same curriculum, then you should try to find a way to get through it all in a year. It doesn't make sense to skip things, especially in subjects like math or grammar, where foundational knowledge is key. It would be cruel to not ever get around to two-digit addition and then expect your child to know how to multiply two-digit factors the following year.

There are also some significant differences between public

school textbooks and some homeschool curriculum options when it comes to repeating things. You may notice that the first few chapters of a public school textbook repeat what was learned at the end of the previous year, and this makes sense. There have been studies documenting the effects of "summer slide," where kids lose some of the skills they obtained during the school year simply because they get out of practice. Don't assume that this is the case with all homeschool books, however. Many publishers waste no time or printed space rehashing what was taught before, especially since many homeschool families don't take the whole summer off. Don't presume there's always an overlap in lesson goals vis-à-vis public school textbooks.

2. Is There Too Much Time Spent on Unnecessary Review?

To me, the best definition of "unnecessary" is worksheets or practice questions for a concept that your child has already mastered. An example would be learning to count money. Some math curriculum options teach money four to five times over the course of an elementary career. If your child is a pro at making change and counting cash, is there really a need to go there again? Maybe not. Skipping lessons your child has already mastered also gives you more time to finish the more challenging ones.

3. Does My Child Just Need More Time?

This is a question that doesn't always get answered in the battle between the "finish the books" and "skip all the things" crowds. Every child is unique, and even if yours has blasted through grades one through three of grammar, they may stumble a bit when they get to grade four. Does this mean that you just push them through to complete the year on time? Are you racing to the finish so that you can cross grade four off your to-do list? Please don't do that.

Homeschooling can be superior to other educational means, but only if it's used to personalize the learning experience to your child. If you just rush them through to hit your planning goals, you could miss out on opportunities to nurture them in their learning difficulties—or worse, make them hate schooling. By all means, if you're not going to finish this year's math textbook because you're doing everything you can to make sure your child learns what they can, just accept that you won't finish. That's perfectly okay.

4. Can We Learn through the Summer?

Ask just about any longtime homeschooler what they're doing during summer break and you'll hear things like "visit Paris!" or "work in the garden" or "summer camp." They're just like every other human in the world. They like the change of season and the possibilities that summer brings.

There's another thing you'll hear among their plans, however: "school." Yep, most homeschoolers keep right on homeschooling through the summer, even if it's not on their agenda. Summer is a great time to do what we like to call "catch up." If we didn't finish that math textbook and know that the next year's book doesn't do any reviews, we'll scramble to get all of that done in the summer months, and maybe throw in some extra reading, too.

Summer homeschooling can be done a number of ways, and it's a perfectly suitable option for the "What if we don't finish our textbook?" dilemma.

A note on reviewing for confidence: In reading the advice above, it may seem like homeschooling should be done for maximum efficiency. It's easy to get into that mindset, since we're busy people with busy lives. Homeschooling is in our hearts, but it also takes its place among so many other things, like family, businesses, careers, and hobbies. I don't want to give you the impression that you should cut out all the extras and make your schedule as lean as possible.

With this in mind, what do you do about the endless review that some curriculum options present? Is it ever a good idea to do more and more math worksheets when your child has already mastered a concept? It can be. For one, it can boost confidence in learners, especially if they struggle in other areas. A child who's slower to read may simply crush their math homework. Giving them all the practice and enrichment pages in a workbook—even after they've demonstrated mastery—may help them to gain that much-needed belief that they can do hard things, too.

It can also just be pleasing for them. I have a child who would like nothing better than to do endless multiplication worksheets. This would have been weird to me as a kid; I hated math. But this is his happy place. And, of course, reading is a favorite for many children. Doing all the work is what he enjoys, and homeschool should, after all, be enjoyable. Don't forget the role of joy in your homeschool, even if it comes in the form of yet another systematic review page.

DON'T LET YOUR PLANNING
BE A SOURCE OF DISCOURAGEMENT

If there's one thing I tell new homeschool parents again and again, it's that you should try to show your child as much flexibility as you can without sacrificing the core of your education or reinforcing bad habits. It's one thing to let a couple of math weeks slide because of a death in the family; it's another thing entirely to do the same because your child has discovered online first-person shooter games.

I'm as guilty as the next parent of not always being as firm with my kids about staying on task. (I'm a procrastinator myself; I get my best work done at the last minute.) When it matters, however, I can hold my kids to a deadline, especially when it means giving them access to important opportunities. This is why I'm firm about things like studying for the ACT or getting research done for a team speech project where other kids rely on them for their success.

Even if you decide, against my suggestions, to plan every day of the year out in advance of the new school year, I recommend you write in pencil. I also suggest you don't tell your kids about your ambitious goals. Do you really want your child to feel the stress of the calendar?

You can lovingly encourage them to stay on task, but try not to let your frustration or disappointment show if you have to scrap that extra art module you'd hoped for. Your kids will take their cues from you as to whether they're succeeding in their homeschool environment. Try to be a cheerleader when you can, and let the calendar take a back seat to new goals and experiences for your child.

In the long run, what they will remember—and what matters most—is not the order of the lessons but the pleasure they take in learning.

Chapter 6

HOMESCHOOLING THROUGH THE GRADES

E very kid is unique, and I'm not just saying that to sound poetic. I've had kids who taught themselves to read at age five and others who suffered through years of *Dick and Jane* books just to get to reasonable comprehension by nine or ten (and then they promptly dove into Dante's *Inferno* like it was a dish of candy). If you've spent any time with your child, you know that they'll likely do things in their own time. Homeschooling is about prompting them when they're ready to try new things and coaching them through it.

Some experts will lay out plans for exactly what you should be teaching your child at every grade level, but these guidelines should only be used as suggestions. In the end, you decide what to teach and when. Here are some various approaches for instructing each age group.

PRESCHOOL AND PRE-K

The experts are torn on whether kids in the two-to-five age group even need to be formally schooled, which means you have even more freedom at this stage. Proponents of the delayed formalized learning camp think kids get enough learning when allowed to freely play and explore up to the age of six or even seven. Others see no need to wait in having them sit, pencil in hand, ready to tackle the three Rs with the same seriousness at the age of four or five. Most of the extant research has been done in formalized school settings, and while there have been notable gains made by kids who start school early, the academic advantages usually flatline in later elementary.[1] Kids who get access to early childhood education often do no better than their late-start peers in many measurable areas, but social and economic benefits do exist for many.

So, what does this mean for you, the parent at home? Maybe you're drawn to the idea of having some structured learning opportunities for your child during the day. Or perhaps you're keener on the idea of letting them loose with a tool kit of open-play materials and all the books they can pull down from the shelf. Many of the parents I know waver back and forth between these two points of view, with most (like myself) falling squarely in the middle.

Happily, there's no shortage of materials for kids in this age group. Some are quite structured, with lesson plans and a verbatim script that you can read aloud to your child. Particularly for parents without a lot of confidence in their teaching abilities, a curriculum can be a crucial support. You may find this the best way to start, and then—as you become more comfortable with teaching—take some liberties with what you actually teach in a day.

For a slightly less structured approach, there are collections of read-alouds (engaging and often popular children's picture books) that have been made famous over the years, complete with some crafts, comprehension questions, and songs. These read-alouds may include Caldecott Medal–winning classics like Robert McCloskey's *Make Way for Ducklings* or Ezra Jack Keats's *The Snowy Day*. You can choose to do the activities that your child's temperament and time allows, and you're always free to skip books or add in your own. Preschool math is generally taught through manipulatives, like little blocks or small toys, which help children visualize the concepts of addition and subtraction and begin counting. Social sciences can be covered through books, especially those that explore the culture of the child's world. (If you have a children's museum nearby, this also makes a great field trip.) Science lessons come from simply exploring the world around them. Nature walks, time feeding the family dog, and observing whether a toy will sink or float in the bathtub are all appropriate "experiments" for this age.

One element of preschool education that's often overlooked is simply teaching children how to interact with the world around them. Sitting nicely at a table, learning to brush their teeth, and using "please" and "thank you" seem like commonsense things to us, but kids have to learn them somewhere. For parents looking for guidance on what social skills they should teach at this age, a good health and wellness curriculum can help, but again, books are often the best tools to teach morals or virtues. Those looking for a faith-based approach can introduce those stories here, too.

KINDERGARTEN

This is the year things start to get serious. While your approach toward teaching doesn't have to change much from the year before, your state officials may require things to look much more formal on paper. The compulsory attendance age for your state usually kicks in around the time kids go to kindergarten, although a few states give you until age seven. Whether you have to fill out the paperwork or not, this is also the age that homeschool curriculum companies really start to push formal learning options. You may also get a call this year from your local public school encouraging you to sign up for classes—or what many homeschooling communities call "kindergarten roundup."

(If you've already decided that homeschool is the only way for you, don't feel pressure to attend these events. Unless you've failed to fill out paperwork for your state and are assumed to be enrolled through the public school, you don't need to do any of the public school orientations either. Double-check with your state's Department of Education to be sure, but it may be confusing for your child to meet with teachers in an environment they won't actually be experiencing. Just politely decline and let the coordinator know that you've filed for homeschool status and won't be attending.)

What do kindergarteners learn? The short answer is "the next things." As homeschoolers, you can allow your child to progress through learning at their own pace, so it would make sense that they would pick up where their pre-K and preschool years left off. In fact, one of the beautiful things about homeschool is that you don't ever really stop learning and teaching. There are very few hard breaks like there are in public school. You may take a break from the spelling lists over the holidays, but since learning occurs in the home naturally, the kids will continue to thrive and grow and get what they need socially and emotionally even if you never open a book during the holiday. The transition from pre-K to kindergarten (and every year after that) will be a seamless blend in much the same way.

Common goals for kindergarten students to be able to achieve include:

- recognizing, naming, and writing numbers one to ten, solving some basic addition and subtraction problems
- recognizing, naming, and writing letters and knowing some or all phonic sounds
- being able to write their first name and possibly their first, middle, and last names in proper print format
- being able to listen to a simple story and tell it back, using pictures, words, actions, or songs to help explain

- know and recognize the five senses, seasons, day/night, living vs. non-living things
- performing basic life skills, such as reciting a phone number, recognizing a birthday, knowing left from right, telling time to the hour on an analog clock, and tying a shoe

(These are all suggestions. Children develop at different rates, and these recommendations can be tweaked to your own students' personal achievement standards.)

ELEMENTARY YEARS

The scope and sequence for grades one through six are largely dependent on you and the method you use to school your child. You may have already picked one of these approaches when getting your pre-K or kindergartner started, but it's also possible that you dabbled in this and that and won't find a need for a "style" until learning becomes more formalized. I actually recommend that parents not pick a homeschool style until they've spent a year or two at home with their kids, especially if their children are very young. You'll be more likely to know what suits them and can save a whole lot of headache and money from buying materials that end up being a bad fit for your kid.

Here are some of the more common approaches to homeschooling, although there are three or four more being created and marketed each year. If you hang out with any homeschool parents, these words will pop up. Know them for the vocabulary term's value, even if you prefer to go with the eclectic method. (Jump ahead to page 85 for more about eclectic homeschooling, which is the method I use, and probably the most popular among homeschoolers.)

Classical

When many people hear the term "classical," they immediately think "old." The classical education movement has existed for some time, but new products and curriculum options are created all the time. Based on the idea of the trivium, a liberal arts concept of learning that dates back to the medieval period, classical ed seeks to teach kids based on their cognitive development level:

- **Grammar stage:** Common for the elementary school years, this stage of classical ed commonly requires kids to memorize facts and master concepts through repetition. For language concepts, this involves listening and dictating back or transcribing; for math, memorizing addition and subtraction facts and multiplication tables.

- **Logic stage:** Kids start developing the ability to analyze and think critically around the middle-school years, and classic ed seeks to deepen their understanding of concepts. Debate is encouraged, as it requires children to know the material very well and speak extemporaneously.

- **Rhetoric stage:** Abstract thinking develops in the high school years, when kids can share what they've learned in their own words, and perhaps even expand on the concepts that interest them.

Some, but not all, classical homeschool programs are Christian in nature. Latin is valued as a language, and students are encouraged to learn Latin as a basis for building English vocabulary and getting a jump on other Romance languages (such as French and Spanish).

Montessori Method

The ideas pioneered by Italian doctor and educator Maria Montessori form the backbone of many preschool and private school programs in the US today. Her methods have become so popular that home educators have also adopted them. This child-centered approach values the child as a unique individual, and learning follows their lead. The classroom is seen as a preparatory environment for the real world, and kids are encouraged to use hands-on methods to explore their world, develop skills for the future (such as cooking or building), and collaborate with other students. Mixed-aged classrooms are standard in Montessori schools, making the method a natural fit for homeschoolers with students of various ages.

Charlotte Mason

If you're just dipping your toe into homeschool circles now, you've probably wondered who this Mason woman everyone keeps talking about is. Charlotte Mason was a late-nineteenth-century British author and teacher who prized high-quality literature and nature. Her methods focus on "living books," or narrative literature that teaches a story, as opposed to textbooks. Homeschoolers who follow Charlotte Mason will spend a good part of their time on "nature walks" with notebook in hand. Art and music are also introduced at an early age, and students do a lot of narration, dictation, and copying to help master facts and concepts.

Like the unit study method below, Charlotte Mason followers can either make their own curriculum by assembling books and activities from various sources or buy prepackaged bundles. The focus on living books means that the library is a popular (and money-saving) stop for these students. Examples of living books commonly used by homeschoolers include *Handbook of Nature Study* by Anna Botsford Comstock (often used for science) and *Paddle-to-the-Sea* by Holling C. Holling (used for geography). Book lists for Charlotte Mason learners can be found for free at AmblesideOnline.org.

Unit Studies

This method of teaching focuses on one subject or topic and explores it through the lens of various school subjects. A butterfly unit study, for example, could include the science of watching butterflies go from egg to caterpillar to pupa to winged creature. For language arts, the children might write about their experience. Math could involve a series of worksheets with butterfly-themed illustrations. History might require reading about famous naturalists who studied butterflies. Unit studies can be homemade, with you assembling the materials from a variety of sources, but some parents choose to buy premade unit studies. Since the focus is the topic, most aren't targeted to specific ages, and can work well for families of various ages and developmental abilities.

Homeschool-in-a-Box

Parents who want to buy a single bundle of homeschool products for a particular age or grade might enjoy using the homeschool-in-a-box approach, which gets you everything you need in one purchase. Lesson plans, readers, workbooks, answer sheets, and tests are included. It's closer to a public or private school curriculum option, and ideal for those who don't want to (or don't have time to) adapt or personalize teaching materials. Examples of homeschool-in-a-box include the LIFEPAC curriculum from Alpha Omega Publications (AOP), a faith-based workbook set, and Time4Learning.com, a completely online, secular option for all grades and subjects. These two examples are the publishers and distributors of their content, so everything will have the same brand. Other homeschool-in-a-box options may collect materials from a variety of publishers and sell them to you as one bundled solution.

Unschooling

Unschooling isn't "anti-schooling," as some detractors have termed it, though the concept is admittedly harder to define than other methods on our list. The common goal of unschooling parents is to let the child guide the learning process. Instead of handing children a curriculum and saying "we will study this topic until noon," unschoolers might ask the child what science ideas intrigue them and then set up a learning environment for the child to explore on their own. Unschooling can be very rigorous, as children are motivated learners when given the chance to pursue their passions. How much guidance the parent offers is completely up to the family as well.

Eclectic Method

Are you intrigued by more than one idea on this list? You may be an eclectic homeschooler. This group is known for an "everything and the kitchen sink" approach toward learning and isn't afraid to use the books or resources that fit, no matter what method they evolve from. Eclectic homeschoolers might use a classical method for a few subjects and then mix things up with unit studies over summer break. Some may stick to one method but mix and match between publishers and materials to suit their learning goals and personal values.

If you hear a homeschooler say "eclectic" when asked what method they use, know that they're probably pretty comfortable with their choices and have integrated a variety of concepts into their learning because they're keen on personalizing the education experience; it's not necessarily that they're afraid of commitment or don't know what's out there.

JUNIOR HIGH AND HIGH SCHOOL

Barring any emotional or cognitive obstacles your child may experience, this age group should be able to work independently on most of their subjects each day. I've created a suggested scope and sequence you can refer to in Appendix B to help you know what they need to learn, but that will also depend on whether you're preparing your child for college, trade school, or the family business. Chapter 13 goes into the details of prepping your young adult for the real world. At a minimum, expect your sixth- through twelfth-grade parental responsibilities to include:

- picking a curriculum for each of the required subjects and extracurriculars
- becoming familiar with the scope and sequence of each curriculum
- creating a plan or yearlong schedule, with milestones, according to the tips in Chapter 5
- setting up some weekly goals for your student to meet to stay on track
- checking in at least once daily to see if they have questions and that they're doing their work
- being available to field any questions, and reaching out to other resources if you can't answer them yourself
- checking and providing feedback on tests or writing assignments, if this isn't handled automatically by the curriculum or course provider
- giving encouragement when your kids take initiative and do their best work; providing consequences when this doesn't happen

You'll also want to use these years to identify your child's particular gifts and talents, and how they may align with a future career.

ADDITIONAL HELP BY SUBJECT

I've picked up a few tricks over the years to get more learning in with less time and fewer tears. Here are some additional thoughts on learning by subject, with some extra hints for giving you the best experience.

Reading

Parents get more panicked over whether their child can read than almost any other developmental skill. This is understandable, since it's such a concrete milestone, and it's hard not to compare your kid's progress with others'. But before you stress over it, know that—barring any significant doctor-diagnosed issues—your child will get there. I compare reading to potty training: it can be rough going for some time, but they all eventually get there in the end.

Whole Language vs. Phonetics

Depending on when you went to school, you probably remember learning to read differently than I do. My reading came naturally, at age two, with a phone book on the living room floor. I remember phonetically sounding out letters from *Sesame Street* and *The Letter People*. Phonetics was the method of my generation. We learned each letter had a sound (or two), and we strung together sounds to create words. It was codebreaking for preschoolers.

Then came whole language, which had roots going back to the eighteenth century but didn't rise to popularity in American schools until the 1980s and '90s.[2] This approach aimed to teach kids how to read based on the meanings of entire written words in the context of stories. If you saw the word *bed* enough times within a story about sleeping, you would recognize the word again each time after that. It allows the child to default to phonics when they encounter an unfamiliar word, but the goal is to learn as many words as possible.

Which is better? I've been partial to phonics my whole life, because I can't imagine how I could teach my kids every word they'll need to know. However, the English language is a nightmare to decode, and there are so many exceptions to the phonics rules that whole language can't be discounted. Personally, I use a phonics program that incorporates "sight words" to help speed the reading mastery along, and to also keep my kids from melting down every time they meet yet another word like "cough" or "knife." If you pick a side, rest assured that most of today's homeschool reading programs are designed to handle the nuances of the English language, regardless of their dominant method.

Encourage Natural Reading

My ten-year-old went a full year wanting to read everything on the back of cereal boxes, including nutrition labels. Then it was canned goods. What started out as a slightly annoying habit became fertile ground for improving his vocabulary and helping him master more complicated words. Embrace any opportunity for your kids to read, even if it's weird or inconvenient. You never know when sounding out "contains no monosodium glutamate" will be needed in the real world.

Read at Bedtime

You likely have to tuck smaller kids in anyway, and the fifteen to twenty minutes before they crash is just enough to get in a chapter of *James and the Giant Peach* or another book required by your homeschool curriculum. Bedtime reading gives them good, warm-and-fuzzy memories of books, something that can help them become adult readers; it's also a good way to knock out those "lit" requirements. This is great for kids who share a room and are close in age, or who can't always get together during the day for a group read-aloud.

(A word on *James*, however; it—along with several of those childhood faves—has some mild gore. If it's been a while since you've read one of these older books, give it a go-through before sharing with the kiddos. While some of the scary themes we accepted in classic books from our day are manageable during the daylight hours, hearing about one of the aunts being squashed flat by produce can be the stuff of nightmares. If you have sensitive kids or fitful sleepers, keep the evening reads lighter.)

Have Them Read To

If you have older kids in the house who can read, you have everything you need to get those little ones a proper literary education. Having siblings read aloud to the younger ones isn't just a game-changer that saves you time and frees you up to do all the other things you need to do; it also creates empathy between kids. The bonding you feel when you read to your child can and should be encouraged among siblings. Whether it's a single picture book or a set "twenty minutes of afternoon book time," take advantage of this perk of having multiple children.

Watch TV with Subtitles

As I get older, I find it harder to hear, and watching British television almost always requires me to turn on subtitles. Closed captioning is beneficial for even those with perfect ears, and putting those little words on the bottom of kids' shows gives children another way to comprehend the English language. Subtitles are a benefit for foreign-language learners, too. Many of the popular kids' TV shows have the option to turn on words in French or Spanish!

Apps Are Okay, Too

Mobile devices have a bad rap among those of us who use them to crush candy or get chickens across busy roads, but tablets and phones also offer fuss-free ways to get in some lit units and shouldn't be ignored. Whether you load up your Amazon Kindle to help kids read while waiting at the doctor or invest in one of many high-quality phonics apps, screen time can be a palatable way for kids to polish their reading skills without tears. Apps we've used with success include Reading Eggs and Khan Academy Kids.

Math

Depending on the math program you choose, you may have to invest in manipulatives. What are they? Manipulatives are concrete objects that help reinforce abstract math ideas. For a child, it can be hard to grasp that a written equation is a symbol for something real.

Much like word problems (Adam has five apples, etc.), manipulatives give concrete form to the numbers.

Luckily, manipulatives don't have to cost much. Some of the more expensive math curricula come with blocks or bricks or tiny toys. I love these products, and I see them as a great investment, if they make sense for your budget. If they don't, a math program that works with homemade or store-bought manipulatives might be a better fit.

Ideas for manipulatives:

- small candies (such as jelly beans), marshmallows, or raisins
- marbles, LEGO pieces, small cars, or beads
- toy money sets from the dollar store
- printed manipulatives that you laminate at home

Please note that manipulatives, by nature, are small objects. Don't use them with children under three years of age or those who still "mouth" objects, as they can be a choking hazard.

Mastery vs. Spiral Learning

If you've done any math curriculum shopping at this point, you may have heard the term "mastery" thrown around in either the description of the materials or in the course's mission statement.

What exactly is mastery? Isn't all schooling aiming at mastery?

If you grew up in the American public school system between 1960 and the 1990s, you probably didn't learn via the mastery approach. You may have even remembered feeling that subjects like math and grammar went around in circles. You may have been introduced to nouns in first grade and likely revisited them again, in some form, every year after that (even doing noun reviews in high school!). This "spiral approach" was the standard for the time, but according to Demme Learning's explanation of the differences between mastery and the spiral approach, US test scores weren't holding up as well as they should have on a worldwide stage.[3] Something needed to change.

That's when most US schools switched to a mastery method. Instead of doing a short session on two-digit addition and moving on regardless of whether you actually understood it, you would spend a whole lot of time on two-digit addition. You would learn as much as you could about it. Then, only after you had "gotten it," you would proceed to another concept—like three-digit addition.

Most textbooks today, especially in math, use the mastery method. Demme, the company that first introduced me to the concept, is a good example. A third-year math student would learn all they could about addition and subtraction, for example, before moving on to multiplication the following year. Then comes a year of division, fractions, and so on, until they're ready for the multi-concept math courses, such as algebra and geometry. This approach is so concept-focused that they don't even name their math levels by grade; rather, they use names like "Gamma" for the fourth year and "Delta" for the fifth. With this approach, there's less pressure to be at a particular point at a particular time. You move on only when you're ready.

Are their criticisms of mastery learning? Yes, but they're easily remedied by doing plenty of review of previous concepts after each new concept. In many textbooks the pauses to reinforce earlier concepts are called "systematic review." If you're interested in pursuing the mastery method and want to ensure your child doesn't go five long years between learning to add and reviewing addition problems again, make sure your math system includes frequent check-ins.

Where to Find Math Help

Whether you were a math wizard in school or not, there will come a time when your child comes to you for help with a math problem and you won't know what to do. This could happen in first grade. (Hey, it's been a while.) It could happen in eighth. Do you have a resource to turn to in times of trouble?

The first thing I would do is check the math curriculum directly. Even if you have your child doing online or video courses, there may be a parent guide with tips for working through concepts. Even seeing how the answer is written in the teacher guide can be useful. If you feel more lost than before, go through the math lesson the child just did. Sometimes, hearing the video instructor explain it is all I need to have that essential aha moment.

Then use many of the free online resources. Khan Academy is still my go-to place for all things math. With the easy search bar I type in "long division" or "Pythagorean theorem" or "cosign" to get the exact lesson and accompanying video for a quick refresher. I don't always even need to teach my child from here; having them watch this Khan video is sometimes enough extra info to get them on their way.

Another neat thing about trying resources outside the curriculum is that it's a different point of view. While I love the math program we use, it sometimes takes a change in language or a different visual depiction for my child to really understand. Pulling up a free Khan Academy video gives that different perspective. It can do wonders for jump-starting stuck kids.

There are a few apps available that claim to give you the answer to problems based on a quick photo snap as well. I can't speak to these, so use at your peril. Expect to see more crowdsourced math resources for parents in the future, however, including app-based methods.

Science

Teaching your child science can feel like an overwhelming task, one that litters your dining room table with pig fetuses and beakers and lab notebooks. The older grade levels can come with some of this (or not, if you go the virtual route), but science can also be a stress-free and beautiful subject for your kids to learn.

Science in the Lower Grades

I admit to not having my kids learn very much textbook-based, formal science in their elementary years. It was something we just never had time for, and I stressed about it until they got to junior high. Then I realized that my kids knew 80 percent of the physical and life science concepts they were expected to know at that point. Aside from some jargon, they were spot-on with how things worked and why the scientific method was so cool!

How did this happen? I think our lifestyle was a big part of it. We live on a four-acre homestead, and "science" was an everyday part of life. My children grew seeds into plants in our garden, raised chickens and watched eggs hatch, helped fix lawn mowers, viewed the constellations through telescopes, collected way too many rocks, kept a bird journal, and watched hundreds of hours of YouTube, *How It's Made*, *Wild Kratts*, and *Octonauts*. From a very young age, our kids were encouraged to explore. My six-year-old would often ask me questions, and when I admitted I didn't know the answer, I would be ordered to "research."

Kids are natural scientists—if you can get out of their way long enough to let them learn. But I understand parents' hesitation to leave things to chance, especially if you don't have a vast wooded river bottom to prowl.

<u>What to Learn When?</u>

Science is a bit like history in that you can prioritize the topics you think are most important in the elementary years, or even take a completely child-led approach. If you choose to forgo a curriculum completely, you'll find Charlotte Mason and unschooling and possibly even Montessori methods to be a good fit. It's also worth noting that many of the high-end classical curriculum providers don't provide science-specific textbooks or materials for kids in grades K–6. Their reasoning? Science is in everything we do, from observing the food we eat to playing outside with friends. Reading books and learning about the world around us is one of the most effective ways to learn science, but if you need to have a schedule for the younger grades, using a curriculum can help make sure you cover the bases so that the middle school years won't be such a jolt to the system. (Check out the cheat sheet in Appendix A for the courses you should cover in middle school and high school.)

One final note: If there's an area homeschoolers may appear weak when compared to public and private schools, it's science. Historically, we've just not dominated in that world compared to other topics. With the explosion in online courses now available, however, we really have no excuse. From coding to robotics to engineering, there have never been more routes available to get your kids on the fast track to a STEM (science, technology, engineering, and math) career. Find out what your kid is into and do your best to direct them to something—anything—that may align with exciting science pursuits. Even if it's just a hobby, scientists really do have more fun.

How Science Can Be Part of Other Subjects

Don't dismiss that science fits naturally into other courses. History, for example, is rich with opportunities to explore how the natural world works. Archimedes, Einstein, Marie Curie, Nikola Tesla, and Elon Musk are just a few of the names and faces kids might meet in their history books. Talking about these revolutionary scientists is a great way to introduce more complex scientific principles and get kids excited about science. Would you rather study a textbook account of how a simple machine works or read about Archimedes's discovery of how a simple screw could be used to irrigate gardens and how it started him on the path to developing a heat ray? I know which one I'd pick!

Literature/Language Arts

Public and private schools have taken varied approaches toward language arts over the years. Many of them, in my opinion, make the subject more complicated than it has to be. Yes, kids need to know what a noun and a verb are. Diagramming sentences can be useful. But regular reading and writing will help kids grasp these skills just as efficiently as any workbook. Whatever formal program you pick, make sure it's rich in literature and long-form writing opportunities.

Literature comprehensive guides are, in my opinion, among the most vibrant ways to learn, and are available from dozens of reputable publishers. These guides are made to be used alongside both old and new "classics," and give kids quick checks of their comprehension as the story moves along. Some guides include handwriting activities or crafts related to the book. One guide for *Little House on the Prairie* included a recipe for cornbread! Now my kids will never forget one of my favorite stories.

High school courses should have more focus on composition, both for fiction and nonfiction. Include plenty of literature here, too. While most curriculum providers have attempted to create a list of must-reads based on the Western canon, homeschooling lets you, the parent, decide what's important in creating well-read, cultured kids. If that's a collection of translated works from your family's motherland, include it. If it's science fiction or Westerns or even graphic novels, go for it. You can swap out books here and there from existing curriculum lists to suit your—and, of course, your children's—values and passions.

While we're at it, spelling is another one of those courses that people seem to prioritize. I have mixed feelings. Some kids are natural spellers and will pick up words from reading alone. Others need daily coaching to grasp even the most basic spelling rules. If you're on a budget but don't want to skip spelling, come up with a simple weekly list method where you introduce it on a Monday, let your kids review it through the week, and quiz them on Friday. It's old-school, but it works! The internet is full of free spelling lists by grade to get you started.

Health

Is your state one of the many that require health to be taught at a certain age? Mine does, although we're free to pursue the health curriculum that best suits our family. Health can include a range of topics, from hygiene and emotional intelligence in the younger grades to sexual health and how to handle peer pressure in the older grades.

With homeschooling, you can choose the approach that meets your values and address each topic as it becomes relevant for your child. For many families, health is less about *what* you teach than *when* you teach it. So, if your five-year-old comes to you and asks, "How are babies made?" and you want to tell them, you can. By the same token, if your twelve-year-old doesn't seem interested at all in such matters but you know they must be taught, you can choose the method that will minimize embarrassment for you both.

You can use videos, books, a formal curriculum (complete with worksheets and tests), or a drive around the block where the kid can ask any question in the world. But if nothing else, having access to a good health curriculum may help you check off the topics you know you need to get to at some point. Even a table of contents from a textbook that aligns with your family values can make a great guide for what to cover.

Social Studies

Let's address the elephant in the room. Social studies (and history, for that matter) is very nuanced, and how you'll teach it depends greatly on your worldview. Culture wars have raged for decades over who gets to tell the stories of our past. In fact, you may have decided to homeschool based on this truth alone.

The great news is that you're homeschooling in a time when your worldview is most likely represented somewhere in the history, civics, or economics courses available right now. If it's not? You can use the eclectic method mentioned earlier to create one. If you don't like the way a world-class history course is handling the Cold War or think there's not enough time spent addressing the Trail of Tears, you can change that. Check out books, watch documentaries, and talk to your kids about the parts of history that have shaped you into who you are today. This is especially useful for first- or second-generation Americans who want their children to learn about their culture of origin as well as the overall American experience.

Do You Learn in Order?

Even if you start with the Big Bang theory and go up until last Tuesday, you won't cover everything. There's just too much there. So focus on the major events, things that mean a lot to your family, and things that your child shows a natural interest in. You can teach them in order if you like, but it's more important that you teach them when it's age-appropriate.

What do I mean? It might seem like ancient Greece and Rome are good places to start, but you won't want to spend too much time going over Nero's torture techniques with a first grader. Best to give a basic idea of that time at an early age, to help with context when they study it in earnest, usually in high school. Many homeschool curricula are structured this way—where your child covers the big events twice—so it's worth checking them out if that appeals to you. And when your child shows a particular interest in a subject, you could spend a summer or a semester doing a deep-dive study, such as the literature of the Holocaust or how the Supreme Court has ruled over the decades.

Whatever you choose, remember the simple rules: Timelines are your friends. Keep a timeline somewhere in your homeschool, with a line from the earliest point in your learning to now. As you study a new topic, mark it on the timeline. There are many free timeline resources online that can help you; this becomes especially vital when you start studying the history of world civilizations. It's easy to forget what people in Greece were doing at the time people in India were doing something else. Timelines keep it all in perspective for your child.

Don't forget the fun stuff! Experiment with the music, food, literature, and art of each time period and culture. This is one of the most enriching and entertaining parts of learning history, and it can be a huge motivator in getting kids to retain information. Even most public schools do this to some degree, but at home you can get as creative as you want.

I'm a firm believer that we can understand people better when we know more about how they actually lived; it's not enough to memorize the date of an event. To create this empathy, you need to help your child put themselves in those people's shoes. Recipes, snippets of film, and audio recordings can make history come to life in a way that will affect them forever.

Physical Education

PE is another course that many states require. However, a recent survey of the Society of Health and Physical Educators (SHAPE) reveals that only one state and the District of Columbia meet national recommendations for physical activity, and only fifteen states have dedicated extra funding for physical education.[4] As schools continue to focus on standardized testing and issue waivers to exempt them from having kids participate in PE, we're seeing commonplace concepts like recess go away.

This is an area where homeschool can really shine, since it's largely about play and flexibility in meeting your kid's needs. What are those needs? SHAPE recommends:[5]

- Kids get between sixty minutes and several hours of age-appropriate physical activity on all, or most, days of the week. This activity can accumulate and doesn't have to be done all at once; they recommend the majority be moderate to vigorous, and intermittent in nature.
- Kids should try to get in fifteen minutes or more of activity in several sessions each day.
- Activity should be varied and age-appropriate. The goal is to achieve "optimal health, wellness, fitness, and performance benefits."

- Long periods of inactivity during the day (two hours or more) are discouraged.

What counts as physical activity? SHAPE broadly defines it as activities that "include exercise, sport, dance, as well as other movement forms."

There are so many tools out there now to help you along, even if you loved to skip gym class when you were growing up. You can purchase a complete homeschool curriculum with exercises planned out for every day of the year, or you might take a more relaxed approach and ask that your kids do something "active" every day for twenty to thirty minutes in the morning, then again in the afternoon.

Favorites I've seen among homeschool families include:

- riding bicycles
- swimming in the family pool
- jumping on trampolines
- playing tag, competing in sprints, or kicking a ball back and forth

If you have only one child, it may be difficult to arrange a variety of options. Remember that some of the things kids do naturally when in a larger space will be quite active. Blowing and chasing bubbles, for example, will cause little ones to work up quite a sweat.

Technology can be useful for keeping your family on track. Fitness trackers and apps can tell you if you're getting enough activity, although simply counting steps might not be enough; trackers that can determine periods of more intense activity work best. Video games that focus on full-body movements can break up the monotony and come in handy during inclement weather. My kids are all fans of the *Ring Fit* equipment from Nintendo Switch. Not only does it gamify fitness but kids learn proper form and posture.

Art and Music

Have you heard that many schools have cut funding for the arts? In homeschool, that's not a problem. No matter the budget, you can implement arts education in all kinds of ways. From simple cut-and-paste activities to musical instruments to a sibling theater company, this is another great area to follow your kid's lead. If you need inspiration, there's plenty online; you can even hire a tutor (many artists and musicians offer this service as a way of making a little extra income). Homeschool learning centers are also popular places to connect with other parents and get access to in-person classes. If you don't have time (or money) for separate art and music classes, use your social studies time to integrate these topics.

I also recommend taking field trips every few months to experience the arts in person. Concerts in the park, museums, a pottery show, or even a quick visit to a mural painted on the side of a building can make the arts seem less like a thing stuffy adults care about and more like the accessible expression that's been embraced by people of all classes, races, and cultures.

WHY I WON'T TELL YOU MY LIST OF FAVORITE CURRICULUM OPTIONS

Almost every single homeschool resource out there offers a list of companies or curriculum publishers that they find reputable. This is definitely a good place to start. Here's why I'm not doing the same.

1. **Curriculum choices should be based on your family's unique values, but they should also consider your needs.** I know of some amazing classical education options that would definitely align with how I want my kids to learn. Unfortunately, they also require many hours of one-on-one instruction that I simply don't have time for as a small business owner. Do I think they're worth mentioning? Yes. Would I feel good about sharing them as go-to resources when even I can't manage them? No. Just because we share the same worldview or approach to math or phonics or handwriting doesn't make them surefire solutions for me and my very hectic life. I want to grant you the same space to decide what will work for you, too.

2. **Curriculum changes.** Not only do companies—even good ones—regularly go out of business, they can also shift their values and objectives. A science textbook I swore by just a decade ago

may have a revised edition by a new author that doesn't cover the topic with the same vigor. New workbook editions may or may not embrace the Common Core standards implemented in public schools a few years back. Some of the literature paperbacks I've purchased from one publisher are abridged, lacking the essential forewords from great thinkers that make them resonate with my kids. Check your editions carefully and know what you're buying.

3. **New options pop up all the time**. Some of my favorite resources are products or books that have been released within the last two years. While many of the most dedicated homeschoolers have been using the same established curriculum options for a decade or more, I couldn't live without an app or workbook or audible recording that didn't even exist when I started writing this book. To create a list of go-to products may lead you to believe that it's not worth exploring new options. I would hate to discourage you from going out and seeing what's available. From courses to podcasts to software solutions, the world is quickly adapting to the needs of homeschoolers, and I'm sure many more amazing things will be launched in the months after this book is published. Why dismiss all those possibilities?

I want you to be free to come up with your own solutions for homeschooling, even if it means trying things that no one has mentioned to you before. In fact, I encourage you to seek out some things that aren't being touted in your local homeschool group.

As much as I love the homeschooling community, they're like any other group, and often look inward for answers. If you have no idea where to start with math, for example, you might ask your local group what they use, and if you hear dozens and dozens of the same answer, you may assume, "This must be the only option that really works." If you try it and it isn't something you love, you may have doubts that you're using it correctly, or even worry that something is wrong with you and your child.

Be bold enough to step away from the recommendations of the crowd. There are so many choices. Even the most expensive, award-winning curriculum products on the market won't work for everyone. Some of my most-loved solutions are made by smaller companies, teachers, or even parents with no connections to the homeschool industry. If you're a fan of "indie" products in any other area if your life, chances are you'll bring that love to your homeschool, too.

TEACHING MORE THAN ONE AND HANDLING SIBLING RIVALRY

While much of my advice so far has been given with a single child in mind, the reality is that most of today's homeschool families are managing the education of multiple children. Whether there are two years between your kids or fifteen, figuring out sibling schedules (and rivalries) can be challenging.

So what do successful homeschoolers do about children with just a year or two between them? If they were previously in public or private school in the same grade, I would continue them in the same grade at home. You can also do this with kids close in age who didn't share a grade. It will take a bit of creativity on your part, but the benefits are worth it, since you'll greatly save on time (and prep) for the courses that require you to be more involved. You can also save on the cost of course materials by making copies. Buying just one math workbook a year instead of two can be the saving grace to an already-tight budget.

Of course, there will always be some sticky situations. Kids can be competitive. Children who come straight out of the public or private school systems may believe that there's a "pecking order" to obey, with the kids in older grades acting superior to their younger siblings. This doesn't always happen, but it's common. One way to nip this in the bud is to make them sit together for courses where learning doesn't have to occur in a particular order.

Areas where you can have mixed ages and stages of kids include art, music, subject-based history or science, health, theology, languages, and even grammar. In fact, math may be the only subject where you have to teach in a certain order—for a few years, anyway—with kids picking up where they left off in the public school system.

Even then, kids who are close in math skills can still be taught together. Some curriculum options teach on more theme-based topics. Math-U-See, for example, is a curriculum that teaches addition one year, subtraction the next, multiplication after that, and so on. It builds on previous mastery, but kids close in developmental age could jump into a year close to both of their skills and learn together. This math option provides plenty of review for the child who needs to catch up and challenging enrichment exercises to keep the more advanced student engaged, too.

Even after you figure out the "what," there will still be struggles. One kid always seems to pull ahead of the other, whether on a single lesson or the entire course. Even if your kids are kind to each other, bad feelings may come up. What can the parent do to challenge one without discouraging the other?

I believe that all kids have unique gifts and abilities, and that homeschooling gives us a handy lens to discover them. If you see one of your children struggling to bloom in the shadow of another, I suggest separating them for one or two subjects during the day so each can shine. Your high-achieving student will probably find all kinds of things that they do well in, and getting them set up with an online course or doing some advanced math or science won't be a problem. The other child, however, might require more personalized attention to discover their strengths. Give them access to things that fall outside the normal school curriculum.

Do they enjoy gardening? Are they a whiz with watercolors? Can they tell an amazing story? Let them establish an identity separate from that of the sibling who seems to excel in everything; then protect that pursuit for a time so that your child can develop and grow without the threat of the high-achieving child coming in and showing them up. I truly believe that you'll find that kid's "thing," something they will do better at than even their high-achieving sibling; it's best to give them time to grow comfortable and gain confidence in it, however, before chancing yet another competition.

WHY I LOVE F.O.B.

Growing up in the '80s, we had half-day kindergarten. Both the morning and afternoon classes participated in scheduled nap time, complete with those little mats we would roll up and store in our cubbies. While much has changed in how our public school systems are structured, my opinion of naps hasn't. I think rest time is essential to keeping kids charged up and ready to learn. It's also not a bad idea for older kids.

In our house, we have "F.O.B.," or "flat on bunk." A carryover from their summer camps, it's a time in the afternoon when everyone, regardless of age, takes a time-out to lie on their beds or the sofa and relax. Younger kids can be asked to close their eyes, if you think that they may actually catch a few zzzz's. Older kids should be encouraged to read or sit and think. This is a time to pull away from formalized, structured activities and just be. We don't allow electronics during this time either; EarPods and music are put away for the short reprieve.

How long you do F.O.B. is up to you. A minimum of twenty minutes works best. Studies have shown that nap time has benefits even for adults, so if you can take advantage of this time to lie down on your bed and rest your eyes, I highly recommend it. It's understandable if the age of your kids won't allow you to take your eyes off them for even a second, but even lying awake on the couch to take some deep breaths can be beneficial. I know I'm a much better mom post-F.O.B. than before.

THE PRINT VS. SCREEN DEBATE

When ebooks started becoming popular, about seven years into my homeschool journey, I was convinced they were the future. Let's consider the benefits:

- Often cheaper than printed books
- Take up almost no space in the home
- Can be easily sorted and organized
- Never really go missing
- Can be read over and over with no wear or tear

If you consider these perks, why would you ever want to use traditional books? Well, they have their own advantages:

- Beautiful and have cultural significance
- Enjoyable without power or additional tech devices
- Easier on the eyes for some kids
- Readable no matter how technology changes

You may hear people favor one strongly over the other, even though most homeschools have a little of both. Is one truly better than the other from a learning perspective? Studies are mostly inconclusive, but there is a slight advantage to printed, physical books that might matter for your family.

A notable study admitted that printed and screen books measure about the same in terms of reading speed.[6] Kids can sit down and enjoy *Diary of a Wimpy Kid* in print or ebook, and they'll likely get it finished around the same time with each. Where print books win is in comprehension and timed reading events.

The same study showed that kids had better metacognition when using printed books, but they also seemed slightly less confident reading from print. Don't we want our kids to be confident? Yes, we do, but we don't want them to be overconfident. When reading from a screen, something in our brains underestimates the attention and focus needed for comprehension. We might skim or cruise through a passage without the same care that we would with print. Books demand our attention, and for many readers they bring out the best reading habits and focus. If your child is considered a strong reader but is underperforming, consider whether ditching ebooks may help.

Other studies suggest that when reading with a time limit, such as during a standardized test, print may have an advantage. Given this information, it may be worth it to pick printed test formats for your student, at least on exams that really matter.

Printed Ebooks and Workbooks

There's another place in the homeschool world for ebooks, and that's printable workbooks and worksheets. These resources are called "consumables" because your student uses them once. Some publishers offer digital versions of their textbooks and consumables, often at a lower price than their hardcopy counterparts. These ebooks aren't really made to be read; you'll print them out and use them to write on.

Before you go ordering all your workbooks in digital format, here are some more facts to consider:

- Depending on permissions, you can often print multiple copies of ebooks to use for more than one family member.
- Some ebooks have watermarks, which can affect the look of the printed product.
- Licenses for ebooks may last for a year, a few years, or forever.

The key to knowing whether an ebook is a good deal is to see what the usage rights include. Most publisher websites should list the usage rights in their Frequently Asked Questions or Terms pages, but reach out if you're unsure (there should also be a customer service number or email). Some publishers are very generous with their usage agreements, letting you make infinite copies and hold on to the ebooks forever. Others may allow you to download the book only once and limit your use to one student.

Remember, just because you *could* feasibly share a downloaded ebook product with friends doesn't mean you *should*. If we want the best publishers and creators to stay in business, they need to earn a living. Making unauthorized copies or sharing digital downloads cuts into that living. Remember that many publishers are small, one-family businesses, many homeschooling their own kids. It's also against the law to make copies or share rights with those who haven't paid for them.

Always back up ebooks or digital curriculum materials to both your computer and a secondary backup source, like a cloud storage provider or external hard drive. If the computer you downloaded it on crashes, you may not get it back. That's money wasted and a real shame for the frugal family.

HOW TO MAKE A SPACE FOR YOUR HOMESCHOOL

Space truly is in the eye of the beholder. I have a 1,300-square-foot ranch home with no basement or attic, and my six kids have been crammed in (along with thousands of books) for over a decade. We joke that we can't be hoarders because our stuff moves to a new location daily, and I truly do make an effort to dust. In all seriousness, though, we aren't minimalists. It can be hard to surround our kids with good books and still provide them with a place to be alone and enjoy those books in such a tiny home.

But here's the thing—I've heard the same complaint from

friends with four-thousand-square-foot homes and one kid. I've heard it from tiny-home owners and RV-schoolers. It's an American affliction—none of us feel like we have enough space.

But stop and consider what you actually need. Even if you were to add on a spare room, would you really use it to homeschool? (I wouldn't. I have three boys sharing one bedroom!) Homeschooling is such an immersive experience that it really doesn't need to be done in a separate space at all. Places people homeschool successfully include:

- the kitchen table (the #1 pick, by the way)
- their bedrooms
- the family library or study
- on the couch
- in a makeshift closet office
- on the porch or patio
- in a car on the way to an event, class, or activity

See a pattern here? Homeschooling can be done anywhere, provided it:

1. **Allows the child to focus.** Some kids need only to be facing away from other kids to get the job done. Others may need it to be perfectly quiet; noise-canceling headphones can sometimes assist in this measure. Still other kids need to be in a different part of the home completely.

2. **Offers a stable writing surface.** Kids may love to snuggle up on the couch to read a book, but this location is inappropriate for handwriting or art. Make sure they have a desk or part of a table that's flat and smooth so they can do their best penmanship without stretching or reaching.

3. **Is ergonomic.** You don't need to invest in a $1,000 standing desk or pro gaming chair to accomplish this. But little people do need shorter chairs, and dangly legs and hunched shoulders will harm your kid over time. Figure out how to give them a comfy workspace on the cheap (hint: IKEA is your friend) and you will have performed one of the hardest tasks of the homeschool parent.

4. **Doesn't stress them out.** Kids can, admittedly, get freaked out about anything. You certainly shouldn't cater to your kids 100 percent, but you should be sensitive to how they learn best. You want to set your kids up for success, so their workspace should be as stress-free as possible. Whether this means it's away from loud pets or not near where other kids are watching TV or out of a busy traffic area of your home, it should be a place kids can really buckle down without having to worry about what's going on with other family members.

(If you have a particularly sympathetic sibling who feels they need to tend to the baby's every cry, for example, don't put this child's work area near the nursery.) What stresses one child may not even faze another, so take these personality differences into consideration when figuring it out.

5. **Makes you look (reasonably) good.** I'm not about to tell you that you should try to be someone you're not. If your home is cluttered or you tend to squawk at your little ones from the other end of the house, you're in good homeschool company. Since some homeschool courses are done through live online learning classrooms, however, you should consider how your home will appear via Zoom or Adobe Connect. Optics do matter. Homeschoolers already have enough scrutiny without people getting a peek into our very private home life. This may mean having your child tidy up their space before class starts or instituting an "everyone wears clothes by 10 a.m." rule. Not only do you not want to attract attention from the school, you don't want to be a pest to the rest of the virtual students trying to focus and learn.

{ *Chapter 7* }

PAYING FOR HOMESCHOOL

I f you like the idea of homeschooling but are concerned about cost, I have good news for you. While you may have to shuffle your work or your childcare worlds around in order to oversee your child's education (and that, certainly, could cause a change in the budget), the actual price tag for homeschool materials can be very affordable.

I've seen dedicated parents do it for practically nothing, paying only for basic school supplies and internet access. (Make sure you have a library card, too, of course!)

Others invest in a formal homeschool curriculum, supplement with a modest library of classic paperbacks, and pay separately for piano lessons or a casual flag football league.

Still other families go the most expensive route: live, online courses for everything from algebra to Latin. They pay for speech club, overnight trips for volleyball tournaments, and private art lessons.

So there's a broad range of possible costs. Multiple children may cost more (although family discounts on curricula and supplies are common). Classes in a city will likely be more expensive than those in rural areas, based solely on the cost of living. I've seen everything from $600 per child per year for homeschool to $3,500 per semester per child, not including extracurriculars and hobbies.

What does the research say? A 2010 National Home Education Research Institute study showed that the average spent per student per year, for everything from books to testing to coaching, was $400 to $599.[1] The study also determined a strong correlation between the amount spent on a student's education and their performance. At almost every grade level, when more than $600 was spent in a given year, that student outperformed peers who received less funding.

Speaking as a mom with a freelance business, we certainly have had our good years and bad. I've spent far more during some years than in later ones, especially as the children grow up. I am not of the opinion that a preschooler needs the same level of homeschool resources as a twelfth grader. I've increased our budget per child as they've grown, and as our income has increased. I've also been more than prepared to cut down to only the basics in years when we've had unexpected expenses or wanted to pursue more important financial goals. (Our very first year, our kindergartner got by with one-dollar workbooks from the Dollar Tree. It can be done.)

Here are some tricks I've picked up through my own experiences, as well as things I've learned from other budget-savvy families over the years.

CONSIDER SCRATCH AND DENT

You probably already know that when it comes to buying an appliance or piece of furniture at retail, there's money to be saved by buying the floor model or an item that has been slightly blemished. These imperfections rarely affect the performance of the product, and few people are aware that this same savings principle applies to buying homeschool curricula.

Many of the major homeschool publishers offer "scratch and dent" specials on their websites, selling items that are less than perfect for up to 70 percent off the retail price. What's wrong with these books? I've purchased more than a few in the past, and I can rarely find much wrong with them aside from a slightly bent corner or dull cover from shelf wear. Knowing that these items will quickly become very used once my kids get ahold of them, I have no reason to care about these minor flaws.

If you're also a fan of saving money in this way, search the websites of your favorite homeschool booksellers for words like "imperfect," or check out their clearance section. Not every site offers this opportunity; others sell out of their inventory quickly. A quick phone call or email to their customer service can tell you if they're likely to have more in stock soon.

BUY RIGHT THE FIRST (OR SECOND) TIME

Mistakes can be costly, and while new homeschoolers should allow themselves a chance to explore different books and materials without fear, purchasing too much of the wrong curriculum can quickly get expensive. I've done it myself. Seeing a flashy new science textbook, I'll buy it, then see that the same series is offered for all of elementary school. Why wouldn't I buy all of them together from the woman selling them online? Unfortunately, this textbook didn't go over so well with my sons, who found the language dull and preferred reading the biographies of scientists as their texts, before exploring each concept through videos. I ended up reselling these same books to try to recoup my money, taking a small loss and creating more work than I had time for.

If you're truly trying to budget and every penny matters, get a good sense of how a book or resource will work before you invest too much in it. Buying an entire year's curriculum from one supplier or publisher may seem like a time hack, not to mention a sound financial decision—especially if they offer a big bulk discount. But what if you end up changing your mind? Ease into any new program first before spending too much. With many books offering free samples or free trials, it's easier than ever to do.

DOUBLE-UP YOUR KIDS

We touched on the *how* of teaching two kids of different ages in Chapter 6, but I want to reinforce the *why* once more. Not only is it an incredible time saver but it can help with a stressed budget, too. Some courses, like math, must be taught in a sequential manner with a somewhat standard expectation of what is learned in fourth grade vs. sixth. Other classes, such as science or even literature, can be flexible in which years they're taught, within a certain range. To save money, consider pairing up children who are closer in age so that they can learn together. The benefits of this are that you're buying only one reproducible worktext a year instead of two, and if the course is taught through video or streaming media, you can have the kids sit together while they learn, so you're paying for only one course as well. An extra bonus is that you're planning lessons and checking work for only one course—which is much easier than two. (Be sure to check the copyright permission for your worktexts before making copies for a sibling.)

GO WITH A UNIT STUDY

If you're new to the concept of unit study, your bank account is in for a treat. This method of teaching lets students of various ages all learn about one topic at once. For example, someone wanting to do a unit study on earthquakes could use the following ideas to teach kids from a wide variety of sources and pay almost nothing to do so:

- watch a video lesson from Khan Academy
- check out books on the earth and geology from the library
- get free printables and lesson plans from the US Department of the Interior and the US Geological Survey websites
- watch *MythBusters:* Season 14, Episode 3 ("Down and Dirty/Earthquake Survival")
- get lesson plans from the PBS website, including maps, worksheets, videos, and more
- watch *NOVA: Deadliest Earthquakes* with older kids

For a historical angle, research famous geologists. To explore math concepts, show your kids how to measure the power of an earthquake. Have kids write a story about an earthquake for language arts requirements. And if you're feeling creative, there could easily be a messy art project in the offing!

LOOK INTO SUBSCRIPTION MODELS

If you do pay to access a course of software online, be sure to research how it's priced so that you truly save. Many companies set up pricing models that reward parents who buy a full year at a time, often with discounts of 10 percent or more over paying month to month.

Is this truly a good deal? It depends on whether you think you'll use a full year. Some of my kids have needed more than a year to finish a course, while others cruise through in half the time. Kids who finish early save money. Learn your child's pace to see if a month-to-month plan would fit your budget better than a discounted annual plan.

TEACH

If you join a co-op, which is a common homeschooling approach, you may be expected to teach at least occasionally. This is often the only way such volunteer organizations can keep everything running. If it's a for-profit endeavor, however, there may be some money in it for you. I've seen co-ops pay teachers twenty dollars an hour or more for sharing specialized skills like sewing, writing, or ACT prep. Those that don't pay will usually give you a discount or free courses for your own children as a thank-you. If you don't have teachable skills, ask about offering childcare. Co-ops often provide daycare services for teachers and give a generous discount to helpers. If you have multiple children who attend the same co-op, taking a few babysitting shifts can really rack up the savings.

BLACK FRIDAY (AND OTHER SHOPPING HOLIDAYS)

When we hear "Black Friday," most of us think of big-screen TVs and busy crowds. But did you know that this is often the best time to stay home and do some homeschool shopping? One of my favorite online course providers offers huge discounts on their live and self-paced courses, and I can usually bring down the cost of classes for all four kids from over $1,000 to well under $600.

Even lower-priced books and services can offer deep discounts on this day. I've seen buy one, get one deals and exclusive bundles go on sale for one day only this time of year. In the weeks leading up to Black Friday, explore your favorite homeschool suppliers' social media accounts and web pages to see what's being planned for the big shopping event. (And be sure to check Cyber Monday as well, since some products that are sold mostly online have shifted their sales.)

EDUCATOR DISCOUNTS

Are you a teacher, or aren't you? It often depends on who you ask. Educator discount programs at places like office supply stores, computer manufacturers, and even coffee shops have been increasingly open to home educators over the last few years. The discounts might not seem significant, but every bit helps (especially if you're a daily visitor to the coffee shop!). Be prepared to show your homeschool paperwork or a homeschool educator ID for some programs. (IDs are available from select companies and advocacy groups for a small fee, although they aren't valid legal IDs. Do an internet search to find places to buy.)

LIBRARIES

Need I go on about the perks of libraries? In fact, I'm always surprised at how many parents are unaware of the full range. If you haven't been lately, stop in to your local branch and ask the librarian what programs, resources, and events they have for homeschoolers. If you live in an area without many homeschooling families, they may not have anything formal set up. But chances are, they have loads of experience ordering books, hosting coding camps, and giving homeschoolers a place to hang out and belong. The free Wi-Fi and books are just the beginning; libraries are also amazing places to buy used books at their annual book sales. (You'd be surprised how many people pass over the classics and other items home educators are pleased to scoop up!)

EMAIL NEWSLETTERS

I don't recommend clogging up your in-box with every sales newsletter out there. I do suggest you get on the email list of the brands and publishers you use often. These are useful to alert you to free shipping or small discounts on items from time to time, but they can also let you know about new products. Clearance sales and "last-chance" buys on discontinued items are more reasons to sign up. Use an email address you won't mind filling up with deals—

consider creating a new one, if you have only one—and remember to check your spam or promotions folder regularly so you don't miss the best offers.

SOCIAL MEDIA PARTIES AND VIRTUAL CONFERENCES

Do you use Facebook or Twitter? Homeschool brands and organizations frequently get together with parents and experts to virtually hang out and share tips. These same social media parties come with prizes, which means free stuff! There are usually exclusive discounts for partygoers, too.

The same type of camaraderie and swag is available at many of the virtual homeschool conferences popping up these days, like those put on by Great Homeschool Conventions and curriculum publishers themselves. They feature expo halls similar to the ones you see at in-person events. From free shipping to gift cards, it's worth it for the frugal family to check out.

THRIFT STORES AND GARAGE SALES

A good 30 percent of the readers and literature books we own came from our hospital auxiliary thrift shop. Another 20 percent came from an estate sale that was quickly liquidated at the nearby collectibles store. Still more I acquired from various garage sales.

You get the picture. If you're willing to pick through old toys and clothes, there are some school treasures waiting to be found. This tactic is good year-round, but not ideal for when you need an item quickly. You never know when that special edition of *Black Beauty* will turn up (if at all). If you're willing to buy when you can and pick up things along the way, you can spend pennies for some excellent materials.

PINTEREST

Why spend twenty dollars or more for a craft book or educational ideas manual when there's so much to be found for free on Pinterest? If you've not visited lately, the site is jam-packed with home educator ideas, free printables, recipes, parenting tips, and product reviews. I've set up several Pinterest boards for the various things I've found, and I sort by need to help me find them later. This is an especially good resource for creating unit studies, as some parents have already done the hard work and assembled everything on their own, single-subject boards. Just search for the unit (or general category) you have in mind and see what pops up.

WORKSHEET GENERATORS AND SUBSCRIPTION SITES

If there's one investment I recommend all families make, it's in a solid worksheet resource site. Yes, you can probably find hundreds of free worksheets and printables online, but finding just the right one for your needs at the right moment can be time consuming. I don't have time to scour the corners of the Web for such things, and you probably don't either.

That's where the worksheet site comes in. There are many available, with some of the bigger sites offering tens of thousands of worksheets. Most work on a membership model, sharing a monthly or annual fee for access to as many worksheets as you can print.

What can you find here?

- coloring pages and "just for fun" activities
- literature guides
- holiday printables, decorations, and puzzles
- reading comprehension units
- handwriting sheets and copywork projects
- math facts and "generators" that let you create unlimited pages of random math problems
- mini posters and books
- planning pages
- reading lists and suggested guides

And on and on and on! A well-done worksheet site like SuperTeacherWorksheets.com can help in so many ways, from helping you find busywork for your toddler to do while you're on a work call to filling in as the worksheet content when you can't afford that more expensive "official" workbook for a course. I've found the cost to be well worth it, and I try to stay subscribed to each one every year.

LINKEDIN

Are you a business professional or small company owner who uses LinkedIn Premium? This service isn't cheap, but it's something I have to have for my freelance writing business. Imagine my delight when I learned that it comes with free access to the LinkedIn Learning platform. Designed for professionals, it also includes hundreds of courses for tweens, teens, and college kids to enjoy.

Courses include photography, 3D design, illustration, drawing, guitar, Microsoft Office suite, and marketing communications. While I wouldn't let your child use it completely unsupervised (it's designed for grown-ups, after all), having a trustworthy student take a course here and there for extracurricular credit can be an excellent money saver for existing subscribers.

KHAN ACADEMY

Khan is a go-to for many things in our home. It's perhaps the only learning site that's completely, 100 percent free and full of courses designed specifically for kids and schools. You don't have to use the full courses, either. We frequently search the site for just one concept (like dividing fractions) and have the kids review with videos before resuming their regular coursework. It's also an excellent way to do PSAT and SAT test prep, with the same quality drills and practice exercises as many of the services that charge $200 or more!

(Khan has also introduced a pre-K and kindergarten app that's quite good. If your little ones are already spending a lot of time online, consider redirecting them to something educational.)

MASSIVE OPEN ONLINE COURSES (MOOCS)

MOOCs may have a funny name, but they are a seriously effective way to save on your child's education. Massive Open Online Courses are offered via the internet by some of the top colleges and universities in the country. While some are asynchronous (meaning you take them at your own pace, at any time), others must be completed in a shortened block, usually eight to twelve weeks. Courses may offer credits or certificates of completion for an additional fee, but even if you only work through the lessons without grades (called "auditing"), your child can get a lot out of these classes.

What's taught? The range is impressive, including art history, programming with Python, Chinese, contract law, circuits and electronics, and Shakespeare's life and work. Your child will learn alongside dozens of other very engaged students. Some courses include forums or interactive components; in courses where you pay to get credit, peer-reviewed assignments are common.

Now, I do need to caution parents that any course taken through a MOOC platform should be carefully researched before enrolling, and kids shouldn't be left on their own to work through them. Because these are college courses, with content targeted at older kids and adults, the topics may not be appropriate for your child's age group or your family's values. It's one thing to have your child come across some provocative lessons as a twenty-year-old; it's quite another to do so at thirteen. Even if your child is very mature, read the reviews of courses for perspective before you enroll. Don't hesitate to drop the course if it isn't right for you. You picked homeschooling for its flexibility, after all.

If you do find a course that works, and your child can progress through it at a reasonable speed, you've not only gotten a college-level education for a topic at absolutely no cost but you've helped your child learn what college will expect from them. While in-person college will naturally be more rigorous, this is an introduction that can motivate and inspire the college-bound child.

SCHOLARSHIPS AND CONTESTS

While you can't bet on winning to fully fund your homeschool, there are numerous opportunities out there to help boost a modest budget. We've been fortunate enough to win two $1,000 college savings plans through our state 529 plan fund, both from coloring contests held in two separate years. Essay contests, photo contests, and chance drawings can offer anywhere from twenty-five dollars in bookstore bucks to tens of thousands of dollars in scholarship money.

Many parents mistakenly believe that the time to look for grants and scholarships is in the junior or senior years of high school, but I think that's too late. Get on the email lists for any organization that offers even small prize amounts, and get your kids involved in a few each year. You never know if you might net some unexpected cash, and the submissions process can help your kids polish their writing or video-making skills in the meantime.

Homeschool curriculum publishers and course providers also offer giveaways and scholarships, often through email or on their social media pages. Requirements vary, and some of the money is given specifically to families who have experienced hardship. If you have your heart set on an expensive live course for your child, it doesn't hurt to ask if they give scholarships. Some may pay only part of the tuition, but every bit helps.

A WORD FOR FAMILIES DURING TIGHT TIMES

Please note that these are suggestions that understandably won't work for everyone. Even the three dollars spent on a monthly subscription may be too much for some families. While investing in your child is a noble pursuit, it's not worth jeopardizing your ability to put food on the table. If money becomes very tight, use what you have or what you can borrow. Learning in its purest form is free. Read books, talk about what you've read, and move ahead with confidence that your child is getting exposure to beautiful ideas, and your love and confidence. These gifts really do prepare a child more for the real world than you would imagine.

{ *Chapter 8* }

HANDLING THE CHILDCARE PROBLEM

Public schools, as we know them, serve two functions in society. They educate, but they're also one of the most common providers of childcare. You only have to scan Facebook around the end of August to feel the angst from parents who just want a break from being the primary caregiver. It's understandable, and it's also one of the main reasons some people will never fully embrace homeschooling. Either they can't or they don't want to be the caregiver and educator for their child (or children) all day.

What happens if you have to work or are a single parent and want to homeschool? I get it. I was a single parent for a few years myself. I didn't homeschool at the time (my child was too little), but the juggling of daycare pickups, coordinating schedules, and ensuring that I could get to work on time in traffic was enough to convince me it wasn't possible for a single mom to homeschool.

Fortunately, many things have changed since 2000. Homeschooling is much more widely accepted, and people are coming up with all kinds of ways to work and raise a kid, even on their own. I won't say it's easy. You'll have to give something up (usually time or money). For those who are living on their last dollar and working three back-to-back shifts, it may not be the time for you yet. I've been there, and I know that it takes outside help or resources just to raise a child alone, not to mention homeschool them.

So, what can you do? Whether you're a single parent, grandparent, or two-parent family with too many obligations, these questions and answers may help move you forward on the homeschooling path.

DOES YOUR CHILD NEED CHILDCARE?

This is a tricky question, because every child matures differently. Leaving an older child home alone for an hour is much different from an eight-hour shift. Having your kid stay by themselves in an apartment with a grandparent next door is different from leaving your kid to fend for themselves in rural America, twenty miles from the nearest neighbor.

You know your kid, and it may be that they can spend part of the day home alone, doing their schoolwork or at least entertaining themselves until you get back to help them learn. It may be that they don't need childcare at all but just someone checking in once a day. You know your situation. Be honest and aware of any state laws that may prevent kids from staying home alone until a certain age.

Can You Hire Help?

Very few of us can budget for the next Tony Micelli to come into our homes and care for the tots while whipping up an amazing casserole each night. Luckily, that's not really what most of us need. There are varying levels of care providers, from live-in nannies to "mother's helpers" to what we used to simply call babysitters. These care providers range in price and performance, and I would use your intuition (and the many reviews on sites like care.com and urbansitter.com) to research anyone you're thinking of bringing into your home.

If you can manage having someone come in for part or all of the time you're away, you may find that they'll keep you working, and encourage the kids to keep on those reading assignments until you get home to do the real homeschooling.

What Swap Options Exist?

Childcare swaps have been largely informal arrangements until more recently. The "you take Jimmy on Mondays and Wednesdays, and I'll take Lisa on Fridays and Saturdays" routine is something parents have been doing for ages. There's no reason it can't be a significant part of your childcare routine. Sure, it limits what you can do on your days off, but it's free. It's also a very attractive option for working homeschoolers who want to swap with like-minded families. They will want to know that you're okay with Jimmy skipping an Xbox session so that he can study this week's spelling list.

Having Relatives Help Out

Many homeschoolers make it work with the help of grandparents or other family members who will sit with the kids while they're at work. If you already have an arrangement like this for younger children, adding in a few older kids shouldn't be a big deal. In fact, siblings can help with the care of younger children and take some of the burden off Grandma and Grandpa.

Traditional Childcare Options

Don't forget, if it's in your budget, you can find traditional daycare or day camps that will take older kids. They won't help with school, but they'll keep an eye while your child either works independently or gets some fresh air.

Childcare Is No Substitute for Your Guidance

While there's nothing wrong with needing childcare during your homeschool years, it's essential to create clear expectations for when the homeschooling will actually get done. As you've read in earlier chapters, younger kids need fewer than two or three hours of formal schooling a day, and that's possible to do when you get home from work or on the weekends. Older kids, while needing more time for schooling, can also work independently. If you have them at Grandma's, for example, there's no reason they can't be reading for Lit class, studying their math flashcards, or watching an online science lab.

Define who will watch the kids, who will teach the kids, and whether those two categories will overlap. In the end, homeschooling is something you chose because you wanted to have input into your child's learning and be able to pass along your values and educational priorities. If you have someone else watching your child, there's no guarantee that they will also do the teaching. Even if your child does 100 percent online coursework, you'll still need to provide oversight, direction, and guidance to keep them on track. As the parent, the buck really does stop with you.

Chapter 9

HOMESCHOOLING AND THE FAMILY BUSINESS

I've told you a bit about our family situation, which is fairly common among homeschoolers—one or both parents working for themselves. It's not easy, but in the best scenario, it does offer you crucial flexibility, especially if you're educating multiple children. Let's take a look at how some other entrepreneurial families have managed it.

TAMI BOURLAND, PIANO TEACHER

Tami Bourland is a piano teacher who decided to homeschool her kids after she noticed her son did better with her around. "I just thought, 'I like having you home, and you like being home, so let's homeschool.' I enjoyed it from day one, so I just continued with my other two boys."

Her piano lesson business allows her to spend the day with her kids and teach piano in the evenings. Tami says that, with a traditional public school arrangement, she wouldn't see her children very much.

JOANNA COMPTON, ICE CREAM SHOP OWNER

Joanna's family has owned an ice cream shop for the past few years, but she isn't new to running a business. Her family chose homeschooling when their oldest daughter reached school age, as they were living overseas as missionaries and the local private schools there were out of their budget. Upon returning to the States, they continued to homeschool through job searches and readjustment to stateside life.

Joanna started a Pampered Chef consultant business while her husband took a job at a church. She worked in the evenings, he during the day. They alternated parenting duties.

"For the kids and I, we did the majority of our schooling in the mornings. While they were still young enough for naps, I worked on paperwork and phone calls during that time. Once they were a bit older and weren't napping, they had 'room reading time,' outdoor play, and some independent computer time, which freed me up to do my work," she explains. Joanna also credits her covered porch as an incredible tool for her business-homeschool balance. "I could work from there while they played in the yard."

When the children got older, they could work more independently, and her business bloomed, leading them to open the ice cream shop as well.

ANNETTE, RABBIT FARMER

This business owner always knew she would homeschool, even before her son was born. She saw it as an opportunity to spend more quality time with her child. She took care of other household duties while homeschooling, which meant she never had to pay for childcare.

"There's work I do when he's in bed, like updating my website and listing animals for sale," she explains. As her son grew older, he was even been able to lend a hand. Now a high school student, he spends about five hours a day doing formal schoolwork, including one course at the public high school.

TONYA BOECKENHAUER, CHIROPRACTOR

Tonya and her husband are both chiropractors with their own practice. While she wasn't always on board with homeschooling, she warmed to the idea after learning more about it. They took it year by year, and now their child is in the fifth grade. Her desire to spend as much time with her children as possible was a major motivator.

How do two doctors manage it? She admits that it's tough at times. "My husband and I have a lot going on with our businesses. I'm blessed to work part-time, so we would do school in the morning and I would work in the afternoon."

When her job demanded that she work three full days a week, she enlisted the help of her nanny to teach her children on those days. "The boys are constantly exposed to business," she adds. "It amazes me how much knowledge they have regarding a wide range of topics such as hiring, firing, marketing, etc. They come to meetings with bankers, accountants, lawyers, contractors, and whomever else I'm meeting. I've seen this knowledge translated into an entrepreneurial ability at a young age."

LYNNAE M_cCOY, VIRTUAL ESL TEACHER

Lynnae works overnight, teaching English online to children in China. Her schedule is challenging, as she's often awake and working when everyone else is in bed. She gets off work at 6:00 a.m. and immediately starts getting ready for the day, while her husband leaves for work and her son leaves for private school around 7:00 a.m. Then she starts homeschooling her young daughter.

"We usually finish up around noon. From noon to about three, we take it easy, play outside, and sometimes I take a nap. My son and husband get home around three thirty, which is when I go to bed to get some sleep before work," Lynnae shares.

She explains that her husband is very involved in helping ensure things run smoothly, including helping with housework and shuttling kids to where they need to go after school. "He takes care of all the transportation to activities, which include sports and church. My son also helps a lot with housework and childcare," she explains.

JENNIFER FINK, FREELANCE WRITER

Fellow writer and former homeschooler Jennifer Fink managed to do most of her work during the kids' quiet time, when the younger ones napped, and after they went to bed at night. She also had an older, homeschooled teen come to her house twice a week to watch the children for a couple of hours in the afternoon. She admits that as her work picked up, she found it difficult to balance it all, including the new public school classes her kids were enrolled in at the same time as homeschooling. "I was constantly running between my basement office and the kids on the main floor—and whenever I was with the kids, I was thinking about work. When I was working, I was worrying about the kids," she says.

Fink no longer homeschools, but she enjoyed her time teaching her children and shares that their schedule was different every day. "We were eclectic, and made it up as we went along," she says. She used everything from Teaching Textbooks for math to math games online, some online spelling programs, the ABC Mouse reading app, library books, and documentaries. Two constants that she kept in her homeschool, however, were the quiet time and an after-lunch read-aloud to her kids.

"Primarily, we followed their interests; we gravitated toward unschooling and learning from life."

. . .

From the examples above, you can see that there's no right way to homeschool while running a business. Some people have chosen homeschooling specifically to make it easier to keep their endeavor alive, while others have embraced entrepreneurship to make them more available to homeschool. It's a chicken-or-egg scenario for sure, but I've noticed that the type of people who make either life-style choice are natural risk-takers and driven to work hard for their families.

HOW DO YOU DO IT ALL?

I really dislike this question, but since it's often the first thing people ask when they learn that I run a business and homeschool, I'll do my best to answer it. Maybe it will inspire you to craft your own answer (because people will ask, trust me).

I don't do it all—at the same time, anyway. If I have an amaz-ing day when we get four subjects done with all of the kids (usually math, history, spelling, and reading), I won't have a very delicious dinner on the table. It'll be "make your own omelet night" or "here's some bread and stuff: dig in."

Likewise, if I do manage to get a delicious pot roast on the table, wash up afterward, and run the vacuum, I'm guessing at least one of the kids escaped my attention long enough to skip their history lesson and lose their math worksheets under the couch.

There's also my career. If I'm on deadline for a client who needs a thousand words on the dangers of heatstroke, complete with interviews and a forty-eight-hour turnaround, both the dinner and the homeschool will suffer. It's just the way it is.

PRIORITIES AND EXPECTATIONS: THE DELICATE BALANCE

So, this may leave you wondering how it's possible to homeschool and run a business, if taking your eye off one thing—even for a minute—means it will inevitably suffer. I find that every day is best handled by working from buckets of prioritized tasks. I've also dispensed with the unrealistic expectation that everything will be beautiful all the time.

Here's how to do it:

1. Start by listing all the tasks involved in running your business. If you are in any way successful, there will be a lot! This includes everything you

handle personally; you don't need to list tasks that you pay others to do, but you should include any tasks where your oversight or management of these people requires some action on your part.

2. Next to each task on your list, rank it with the appropriate letter below:
    A. Items that need 100 percent of your attention. If you turn away even for a minute, there will be loss of life, violation of law, or decrease in income.
    B. Items that require your focus, but if someone pops in to ask you a question, no one dies. You may have to recollect your thoughts, but it's a mere inconvenience.
    C. Items that you do because you have to, but you could do them while bingeing shows on Netflix.

3. Take all the A items and put them on a sheet of paper. Put the Bs on their own sheet. Do the same with the Cs.

Now, take a similar approach with the things your child does in their homeschool:

1. List all the things they might do in a homeschool day. You can start with listing their subjects or

activities—for example, math, science, and trumpet. Then, dive deeper with individual activities within these subjects, such as watching an online math lesson, reviewing flashcards, or taking a math quiz.

2. Follow the same A-B-C ranking as above, considering your level of involvement in these terms:

A. The kid can do this 100 percent on their own, in another room if need be (and with the exception of extreme events, won't need you to intervene at any point).

B. The kid might need you to sit next to them to answer questions as they come up or to handle tech issues, such as logging in, advancing slides, or offering feedback.

C. The kid needs you to assist through most of the activity. For small children, this could be reading text or directions aloud and then helping them hold their pen the right way. For older kids, this might look like grading a test or giving feedback on a written paper.

3. Just as you did with the work tasks, create pages with their own A, B, and C lists.

Can you tell what we're going to do here? The level of attention required for your work tasks cannot conflict with the level of guidance your child needs on a task. You can't do two things at once. Multitasking doesn't really work that way.

By matching up "A" business needs with "A" schoolwork, you're getting a framework for what you can reasonably do with a child in the home with you. You're setting expectations that could end in success rather than failure.

We would think it silly to expect a five-year-old who can't read to do three pages in a workbook that's mostly text without any help. So why on earth would we hand them that workbook right before we go into a very important client video meeting? And yet parents around the world (myself included) have done just this, and then have gotten very frustrated when it didn't end well. We can get mad at the kids when it's not at all their fault that we set unrealistic expectations. Only when you match up priorities can you even begin to create a natural flow with your homeschool.

When you're starting out, you can keep these lists on hand all the time to remind yourself what tasks are reasonable at a given moment. Look ahead to what needs to be done in a school day, as well as for your business, and find places where activities naturally match up. If you have more work tasks needing your complete focus on a day when your kid doesn't have much A-level work to do, it might be worth it to let them do unstructured play, watch an educational movie, or use learning apps on the iPad.

Likewise, if you're having a slow workday and have time and attention to give, do it! You'll never regret the time you spend reading aloud to your child or helping them build a birdhouse. Scrolling through LinkedIn can wait; you get to watch your child grow up only once.

Eventually, you'll find your balance and won't need the reference lists. If you have older siblings or a spouse who has some free time, hand off some of the C-level stuff to them if you need to. In the early years, kids really do more of this than you realize. As they grow up, however, the goal is to get them doing almost everything in the A category. After all, aren't independent children who can handle grown-up life what we're all aiming for?

Chapter 10

WORKING OUTSIDE THE HOME

We've heard quite a bit from families in which at least one parent is self-employed. Bloggers, authors, and marketers are common examples—the kind of careers whose flexibility often complements the task of homeschooling.

But self-employment isn't for everyone (or even most people). So what happens if you have a more traditional job? How can you take your existing work schedule and squeeze in the mandatory hours of home education that your children (not to mention most state education departments) need?

While it requires a little more imagination, it has been done successfully by many parents—sometimes even by *both* parents! Let's meet some homeschool families who (mostly) work the nine-to-five grind and manage to get the three Rs accomplished at the same time.

CINDY'S STORY:
TWIN BOYS AND A DOUBLE DOSE OF ENGINEERING

Cindy Kee is a software engineer; so is her husband. While they've each worked on and off over the years, there have been seasons of their lives when they were both employed outside the home and also homeschooling their fraternal twin boys.

"No one knows your child better than you do and truly has their best interests at heart," Cindy told me. "The longer I homeschooled and the more I learned about how kids learn, the more I was convinced that home was the best place for them through the eighth grade. I knew that if I could get them through the turbulent, difficult middle school years, they would have a better foundation—emotionally and socially—than if they had been in school. But I also realized that once they're high school age, they would start to pull away from me as they mature through the teen years, especially as boys."

Their first year of homeschooling (third grade), Cindy's husband was working part-time from home for more than half the school year. She left assignments that she thought they could handle on their own during the day (handwriting, reading, and some computer software), and her husband stayed home with them and helped direct when they were to do their work. Later that school year, however, Cindy's husband returned to work full-time outside the home. The boys were placed in a daycare center during the day, along with other elementary-aged children who were out of school for a session. (Cindy's school district used a year-round, multitrack calendar for elementary school, so this was not uncommon.) The majority of the homeschooling took place in the evenings and on the weekend.

For all their fourth- and most of their fifth-grade years, she stayed home while her husband worked full-time. When her husband lost his job, they both pursued employment, and Cindy found a full-time position while her husband worked part-time from home.

Like many families, Cindy has been very eclectic in her choices, and uses research to discover what materials are appropriate for each boy at each point in their education. Cindy's family isn't religious, and she generally avoided box curricula, so this approach worked best for her.

Her boys were the same age, but because one has learning disabilities, they had very different educational needs. She used the same materials in many subjects (with the exception of math) but adjusted her expectations accordingly. She also found that a good number of read-alouds were beneficial in creating group discussions (as opposed to having the boys each read the same material independently).

- **For elementary:** Cindy highly recommends curricula inspired by Charlotte Mason and Ruth Beechick for elementary-age children—those that encourage lots of "living books" and either notebooking, lapbooking, and/or projects instead of worksheets and tests. (What is lapbooking? Usually contained within a file folder, these homemade "books" contain mini activities and cut-and-paste projects on a single topic. Think of them as a very hands-on portfolio.)

- **For middle school:** When students are ready, no earlier than fourth grade, the IEW has a great writing program. She also found Trail Guide to Learning by GeoMatters to be a great program for a year or two.

As the kids grew older, Cindy took advantage of her computer at work to stay in touch. Programs she used to check in during the day included text and video instant messaging, Microsoft OneNote, and Microsoft OneDrive.

As Cindy's story demonstrates, things can change rapidly! Just when you think you've mastered your work schedule, a job loss or added hours can wreak havoc on the existing schooling schedule. Parents like Cindy know that it's important to be in tune with how their children learn, as well as how long it takes them to master new material. She knew she could fit their schooling in the times between work, and she adjusted her expectations to accommodate both their employment schedules and her sons' individual abilities.

COMMUNICATE, COMMUNICATE, COMMUNICATE!

Cindy was also adept at the art of switching roles as needed to make sure everything got done. Many homeschooling families with two working parents have found that either parent must be able to step in at a moment's notice to handle anything from lunch to language arts. It takes a combination of skill and better-than-average communication to keep everything running smoothly.

Let's take a look at some communication methods that might work for your family. My husband and I have used all of these at some point in our marriage, and they can definitely save the day.

Community Calendar

These are not to be confused with the little day planners you keep in your purse, or calendars that contain personal appointments and reminders. This is a calendar that anyone, at any time, can refer to when needing to know what the plan is for the week. I personally prefer something very simple, like a large whiteboard calendar that hangs on the wall of the family room.

Each month, we mark down all the important activities that need to be noted: volleyball games, birthday parties, family vacations, and doctor appointments. While we can't possibly fit every single little detail onto this community calendar, the "biggies" are always put there for everyone to prepare for. (Note: If you have small children, be sure to put any erasable calendar high up out of their reach; we've had more than one occasion when a curious hand erased all our hard planning work!) You may also decide to use a free promotional calendar (like the kind you get from the grocery store or your insurance agent) as the community calendar. These can be marked with pen for a measure of security!

Planners/Binders

When we first got married, my husband had a three-ring binder for *everything*! His level of organization was intimidating, but it complemented my careless style and likely helped me become a better manager of our home. What I liked about the binder was that it was a cinch to add pages or take them out as our family needs changed. We currently use a homemade household planning binder that we've pieced together from several different planning tools we own. We have pages for meal plans, coursework, financial info, and chores. *If it's important, it's in there!*

For those families who crave a technological solution, I recommend using a basic sharing app like Cozi.com. It's far more functional for those who want to plan down to the last details, and it includes the ability to sync and monitor every moment of every family member's day. You can also use it for meal planning, to-dos, and shopping lists. Just keep in mind that every new feature you use is an additional thing you'll need to track each day; also, it only works if all family members commit to being consistent in updating and referring to it. So, for instance, it might work well when your children are young and only the adults are responsible for updating, but if you expect them to make their own updates later on, results may be mixed!

Email

I don't know about you, but as a journalist, my in-box gets over eight hundred messages a day! It can be impossible to catch every email from my husband. But for most people, email is the easiest way to stay on top of important messages from their spouse about their house and homeschool. To make sure that your messages are handled effectively and nothing goes unnoticed, I recommend the following tips:

- Designate just one email account that you send home-related messages to. Make sure the account can be accessed twenty-four-seven. Also, be certain that the account is owned by you (not a work-related account) and that your privacy can be protected.

- Add all important contacts to the "approved" list of your email provider. You don't want anything getting trapped in your spam folder!

- Not all messages will be urgent; designate those that should be read immediately with a special subject line tag. For example, if the pickup time for your child's band practice has changed, you might use "URGENT: Band Practice Pickup" as your subject line.

- If you'll be emailing frequently, consider special subject line tags for all your messages. To remind your spouse to pick up cereal at the store next week, start your message with "Shopping"; then it will be easy for your partner to filter out all the shopping requests into one list for easy reference.

- Consider creating an email account just for home management and setting it up on all your mobile devices.

Voice Memo

For those of you who still have your landline and an old-fashioned answering machine, this tip works for you! Voice mails can be a reliable way to convey important messages regarding work-shift changes and childcare needs. Just be sure that you check messages every time you return home and that old messages are deleted on a regular basis. And, of course, digital voice services on a cell phone or Skype can be handled the same way.

• • •

These methods of communication are simple, effective, and affordable. Even if you're in a period when only one parent is working, I highly recommend keeping them going. Families who can stay on the same page for all their important activities will avoid some of the hurt and disappointment that comes when messages get lost in the shuffle. This is especially important for families who, due to hectic work schedules, aren't often home at the same time.

A word on social media: If your family is like mine, social media has replaced many of the more traditional forms of communication. While it may be tempting to choose Facebook Messenger or another instant messaging app to communicate, it inevitably leads to your family using social media more. It's very difficult for kids or even adults to quickly check a message and get back to what they should be doing with all the distractions social media provides. So, in my opinion, it makes sense to use a system independent of these time suckers.

Many of the parents I know with jobs have proven that home-schooling and work are not mutually exclusive. It's possible to do both and actually do them well! Because education can be such a uniquely personal experience, you don't have to homeschool like anyone else; finding what works for you is how parents like Cindy managed to keep things in perspective (and actually enjoy the experience).

MAKING YOUR WORK WORK

So just how do you squeeze in these extra responsibilities? I won't sugarcoat it—hard work and prioritization is the only way to ensure success. But a flexible work situation can help enormously. Here are a few ways real parents are making the schedule work.

Work Scheduling

When my firstborn was very young, I was an assistant manager at a fast-food restaurant. I was asked early on in my employment which shift I would take: the 7 a.m. to 3 p.m. shift or the 3 p.m. to 11 p.m. shift. While the later shift almost always had me working more than my eight hours (closing up was hard work), I knew that it would allow me the most time with my toddler daughter. We weren't even homeschooling yet, but it also reduced our daycare costs.

Many parents are given a choice in the hours they work, especially if they've been at a job for a while and earned some seniority. If you're just starting a new job, you may not have as many options, but for many occupations (food service, nursing, manufacturing, retail), the ideal shift for homeschoolers—i.e., the late shift—might be less in demand.

If you do find yourself needing to make the case for different hours, don't simply state that you can't put your kid in public school. Most companies won't understand your choice, and they may be anything but sympathetic. Instead, try to sell your boss on how it can benefit them: Do you have a special skill that would be best put to use on a third shift? Are you able to provide a certification that others on a shift cannot (medication aid, for example)? Is your pay grade lower than those who currently work the shift, thus putting the company in a position to save more overall? The more sound reasons you can give proving a shift change will be profitable for **both** parties, the better shot you'll have at getting what you want. *You will also want to be open to compromise; your preferred shift for half the week is better than no shift change at all!*

Flextime

As companies look for nonmonetary ways to keep their employees happy, flextime (or "flexitime") has become increasingly popular. This practice, which essentially allows for an employee to work a set number of hours almost anytime during the workweek, has helped many families be more available to their children. This has also made it easier for those employed outside the home to formally educate their children.

While flextime details vary (some companies mandate twenty hours per week at a set schedule, for example), the common theme is that as long as your job is completed satisfactorily, it isn't as important *when* it's actually performed. Obviously, many jobs aren't eligible for flextime, and it's still largely a white-collar phenomenon. But if you can swing it, here are some of the perks:

- a shorter commute by starting work before or after morning rush hour (ditto for the evening commute)
- the ability to attend children's doctor appointments, athletic events, and academic outings by making up this time elsewhere in the week
- complementary scheduling with a working spouse that allows for no gaps in childcare

If flextime is a new concept at your company, it may be difficult to formally open the door. One strategy for employees who want to bring up the topic with their boss is to present flextime as an alternative incentive to a living wage increase or performance bonus. (Many employees would gladly take fifteen to twenty hours of flextime per week over even a twenty-cent-per-hour raise.) This proposal saves the company money and may even make you more productive!

Job Sharing

If you're a full-time employee who needs to reduce hours in order to homeschool but wants to keep your position, job sharing might be a suitable work-around. This practice is exactly what it sounds like: two employees "share" a full-time job, often evenly splitting the hours and tasks between them. Many job sharers have some role in choosing who they will share the job with, and this makes sense (as communication and teamwork are what make a job-sharing situation most successful).

Many women, in particular, have found job sharing to be the perfect arrangement for retaining their job when they want to work part-time after having a child. Assuming you aren't in immediate need of full-time benefits such as health insurance or a 401K (which are often not included in shared jobs), the plan can also work for employees who want to reduce their work hours and commit more to homeschooling.

Telecommute

Working from home for an employer is not to be confused with being self-employed, although the two may look very similar from afar. Telecommuting for a company includes many of the same expectations and perks that a physical office would—complete with benefits, accounting procedures, and tax implications. As workers find themselves having to live farther and farther from the urban centers where jobs are concentrated, many employers are realizing that telecommuting can actually boost morale and productivity with little additional cost or oversight.

Not all jobs are eligible for a telecommuting arrangement; anything that requires the special equipment of a manufacturing job, for example, or the face time with customers that drives retail, are not good candidates. Career niches that are generally phone-based or that involve computers, however, have seen a dramatic shift in the number of home-based workers over the past few years. This trend may be the miracle many homeschooling families have long hoped for!

Depending on your particular job, you may not be able to convince your boss to allow you to telecommute 100 percent of required weekly hours. There may also be technical requirements that are difficult to meet (broadband internet, for example, which may be lacking in some rural areas). It's also important to note that telecommuting doesn't allow for you to relax your working habits; many employees actually report that they work harder when at home, in an effort to dispel any myths that they're slacking off in their pajamas.

Telecommuting with older children is a manageable situation, especially if they're using a self-directed homeschool curriculum and you aren't expected to be on the phone for the majority of your working hours. Parents with small children will quickly learn that it's usually not possible to "work" and "parent" at the same time; adding "teaching" to the mix can be an unattainable goal. Telecommuting usually requires parents with tots to have a relative or older sibling step in while they're "at work," and they homeschool and tend to parenting needs during breaks, lunchtime, and outside of work hours.

So how exactly can you convince your boss to let you work at least some of your hours from home?

Start with a few of these tips:

1. **Draft a formal proposal to explain why it will be a win-win.** Show stats, if you can, document-

ing how your productivity may increase, and always tie the proposed arrangement back to the company's bottom line. If others in the company have found telecommuting to be a good move, include their endorsements of your work.

2. **Map it out.** Don't just assume that your boss will know what your office will look like. Offer a photo of your work area (complete with privacy walls, if necessary). If your job provides home workers with company-owned equipment or technologies, show how your office will be separate from your kids' gaming areas and a productive environment for working. Include contingency plans for how you'll spend your time if the internet goes out, for example, and offer ways you can support your teammates while out of the office.

3. **Be prepared for "no."** Very few would-be telecommuters get approved the first time they ask—especially if no one else has blazed the trail. Assume that it will take a few very patient and well-planned-out conversations with your boss to get the green light on any new arrangement; don't ask the week before you plan to homeschool, for example.

4. **Set up a reporting process.** Don't just assume that once you have your boss's blessing that you're

out of the woods. Telecommuting privileges can be revoked at any time, and most home offices are set up on a trial basis. Work hard to show that you can be trusted and that your employer made the right decision. If you aren't required to track efficiency or goals from home, volunteer this information anyway.

Telecommuting isn't for everyone; those who can work it into their daily lives, however, may enjoy a more efficient daily routine and some measure of flexibility that being "at the office" can't provide. And if there's one bright spot emerging from the COVID-19 pandemic, it's that working from home has become a much more familiar concept in corporate America.

Vacation/Sick Time

Many employees enjoy vacation and sick time accumulation for every hour they work, and some companies are very flexible in how that time is used. While it's never my recommendation to be dishonest (using "sick hours" for a personal shopping trip, for example), many bosses have been open to allowing at least some of these unused perks to be utilized in supporting the challenges of family management.

Vacation time can generally be used however you like, including for homeschooling. If your spouse has to work more than usual or the kids need to tackle the final weeks of an already-lagging school year, scheduling some time at home via vacation days can be an amazing opportunity. Since many companies would rather you use your time than lose it (or cash out, at companies that allow it), there is usually some way to bank your unused hours in a manner that's both truthful and helpful to the family unit.

The Family and Medical Leave Act (FMLA)

In addition to any paid time off that you may have accrued, employers in the US are required to offer unpaid time off according to the Family and Medical Leave Act. This federal law protects you from losing your job from absences in the workplace due to "qualified" medical and family reasons, including illness of you or your family members, pregnancy, adoption, and the placement of a foster child. Many employees are reluctant to call on the FMLA as a reason to take an extended leave, perhaps because they can't afford the unpaid time off. If you find yourself in a bind with the balance of child-care and homeschooling and you happen to experience one of these major life changes, it may be an opportunity to take time away from your job with the reassurance that it will be waiting for you when everything settles down.

Not only can you take up to twelve weeks off under the law, your benefits cannot be lost during that time; this is especially useful for the wage earner who also carries an employer-based health insurance plan. If you're considering using the FMLA to help deal with juggling responsibilities at home, it's recommended that you talk to your employer before making any decisions. Some companies (such as those with fewer than fifty employees) aren't required to offer it, and the FMLA doesn't cover minor illnesses or the care of those outside your immediate family.

I recommend looking into whether any of the above solutions

are available to you. The size of your company, the state you live in, your union status, and whether you're full- or part-time will all affect the answer. Be sure to talk with your HR department before planning any major changes to your home schedule, and ask specifically about flextime and remote work policies before starting any new job.

Having a Backup Employment Plan

There was a time when my husband and I both worked jobs outside the home. Our children were small, but teaching them was a priority. I was working a variety of office jobs through a temp agency. My husband was offering support services for adults with developmental disabilities. We managed to ensure that one of us was always home with the children, and we didn't have to pay for childcare by balancing our work plans accordingly.

While mine was a strictly nine-to-five, Monday-through-Friday gig, my husband worked mostly on weekends. It wasn't unusual for him to leave on a Friday afternoon for his job, over ninety miles away, and return home on a Sunday night with forty hours on his time card. While this schedule left him tired upon returning home, we managed to be there for our small family when they needed us.

Even after my husband picked up more traditional jobs in the following years, he kept his employment with the caregiving company, so we always had a flexible employment option at our disposal. Parents may find it beneficial to keep worker status at a part-time job for times such as these. Even if you put in only eight to ten hours a month to stay on staff, it's worth having a backup plan for when times get tough!

While it can seem impossible, this generation of homeschooling parents is proving the naysayers (including the public school system) wrong with their determination—not to mention their happy kids and balanced budgets. You, too, can find a plan that will work for you; carefully consider what your family really needs, and don't be afraid to continually try new avenues of work, school, and home management.

{ *Chapter 11* }

MILITARY HOMESCHOOLERS

any of those who defend our country have embraced home-schooling as a solution for educating their kids. Military homeschoolers are a unique bunch, because they often have a foot in two worlds: the civilian world and the military. While home education largely isn't new to these families, it is constantly changing, since they have to navigate federal, state, and sometimes international law.

What can you expect as a military member or spouse who wants to teach your children at home? Let's take a look at the basics.

YOU MUST FOLLOW THE LAWS OF WHERE YOU LIVE

The most basic homeschooling rule for military members is that your assignment determines your responsibilities. If you're stationed in the US, you're free to homeschool, but you must comply with the laws where you live. If you're stationed overseas, you must comply with any foreign regulations on homeschooling (which may make it difficult—or even impossible—to homeschool legally).

The Department of Defense states:

> A host nation, state, commonwealth, territory, or possession where a DoD sponsor is stationed may impose legal requirements on home-schooling practices. Sponsors are responsible for complying with applicable local requirements and should consult with installation Staff Judge Advocates concerning these requirements.

Because foreign matters are outside of my expertise, change continually, and are extremely nuanced, it's best to consult a homeschool advocacy group that's familiar with the area. An American expat group, if you can find one, may be a good place to start.

Some military installations, such as those in Washington, DC, are close enough to several different metro areas that you can choose which state to comply with. By researching the state and its homeschool laws ahead of time, you can choose the one that's most homeschool-friendly and avoid unnecessary hurdles to compliance.

KATHRYN DILLOW'S ADVICE

Kathryn Dillow, a mother of three and board member of Nebraska Homeschool, was homeschooled herself overseas as a child in Japan. She entered the military as a nurse upon graduation, met her husband, and started a family. Kathryn, like many parents, didn't warm up to the idea of homeschooling at first, remembering how hard it was for her own mother back at a time when homeschooling books were limited and parents had to create much of the curriculum and lesson plans themselves.

But after one of her young daughters had some unsatisfactory experiences at school, a newly retired Kathryn decided it was time to bring her children home. Her son started in the sixth grade and her two young daughters as a first grader and a preschooler. It was a change that took some time to adjust to but worked well given that her husband was often stationed away from home for long periods of time.

She credits homeschooling with helping her first grader thrive even with her father deployed in Iraq. She completed a full year of school in no time. It was also a big benefit when it came time to move again. While her son took more time to adjust (and required a more formal structure), he was able to adapt with time as well.

"Every time they move, everything the child knows is uprooted," Kathryn shares. Homeschooling gave some flexibility for her family to learn the area and new ways of life in the community without a new school every time, too.

Kathryn is no stranger to the stress of reassignment, and between the years of homeschooling and her frequent moves, she picked up a few tips that may help others. She shares them here for those who may not know where they will be homeschooling next year—or even next month:

1. Research Your New Home

As soon as you hear where your next assignment will be, get online and start looking. If you plan to live off the installation and will be picking out your home, you can start figuring out the places you want to live that are near the things you want to do as a family. There's some freedom here, because you won't have to research school districts; your home choice won't be dependent on getting your child into a good school.

In addition to home research, see what the state requires for homeschooling. (Chapter 3 offers suggestions for where to start.) Make sure you have everything needed to file, if necessary. (Don't pack away those birth certificates!)

2. House-Hunting Tips

Homebuyers and renters may benefit from taking a trip to the new area and seeing the place in person. Kathryn's family did their house hunting ahead of time, leaving the kids with family so that they could get it done efficiently. "Find it, lock it in, and come back home," she recommends. Having a home selected allows you to get settled much quicker. "When you arrive, you instantly get to move into the place, get stuff delivered, and set up shop."

3. Start Packing, but Be Strategic

Homeschoolers need access to different things than non-home-schoolers, so be thinking about what you'll need immediately upon arriving at your new home. Three months prior to moving, go through everything and tell the kids to pick five toys to play with, then put everything else away. Keep out anything needed for school, such as the upcoming year's textbooks, school supplies, or readers. (The last thing you want is to be digging through boxes to find the readers you need for the year.) Even if it's summer, pack next year's schoolbooks to be with you in the car; don't put them in packing boxes! This is also a good time to order books and curriculum tools to arrive by August at your new place.

4. Get the Homeschool Area Ready First

No matter if it's your first move or your fifth, it's important to establish normalcy right away with the kids, and this means giving them a place to study. Remember, kids will have a new house, a new neighborhood, new friends, and possibly even new food. The one thing you can do to help them have something not new is to keep their school structure in place.

You'll have forty towers of boxes or more, but if they have their table and basket filled with math and English and literature books, they can start right away. Have the TV set up and a space they can go play and read while you're unpacking. "When you don't have that normalcy," Kathryn says, "it's hard on the kids."

By prioritizing the spaces kids learn and play first, you won't have to deal with the chaos of not finding a pencil or not being able to watch the learning DVD because someone else is on the computer. These things may seem minor, but they can disrupt your child's focus, and if they happen repeatedly, they may cause your child to lose interest in school.

5. Venture Out Right Away

Kathryn also recommends that you don't wait until you're settled to get kids active in sports, music, and extracurriculars. In fact, signing up for everything within the first week or two—even before you move—is best, since the most popular groups may fill up quickly. Start reaching out to your personal connections in the new area, if any, then the homeschool groups you find online. Be aware of deadlines for things like learning co-ops, which may pass in the middle of the move. "Frontload the process of enrolling in activities," she says. "It makes the transition easier for the kids."

You don't have to wait for formal groups or classes to become part of your new environment, either. Make a list of the local places you'd like to explore, such as parks, museums, and historical sites. Aim to visit one a week, to start. Even with so much going on, it will be a nice break from unpacking boxes, and after all, trips like these are some of the best perks of home education.

ACCESS TO DOD ACADEMIC AND EXTRACURRICULAR RESOURCES

What if you want to access Department of Defense Dependents Schools (DoDDS) school activities and courses for your homeschool child? Since October 2018, the Department of Defense Education Activity (DoDEA) has had an equal-access policy that allows home-educated children to participate, provided they give proper documentation and would be eligible as an attending student. The DoDEA Administrative Instruction on Home-School Students contains additional information, several helpful FAQs, and further instruction on how to access programs for your homeschooled student.

A WORD ABOUT YOUR SLO

When you move to a new area, you most likely need to meet with several officers as part of your reassignment. The inprocessing may include meeting with a School Liaison Officer (SLO) whose job it is to see that you're connected to the local school and can get your kids easily enrolled in the system. While SLOs are trained to see homeschooling as just one of the options available to families, they may have no real experience with it. Don't expect them to point you in the direction of the local homeschool groups or have info on how to be compliant with state law. You'll still be on your own to get your kids where they need to be, as SLOs work largely with the surrounding public schools. That's where their expertise lies.

{ *Chapter 12* }

TEMPORARY HOMESCHOOL

We homeschoolers can get pretty jazzed about the prospect of a new parent joining our club. For years, we were seen as the outsiders in many academic circles and may have had few families in our close geographic areas to share resources with. You can imagine the excitement when another family opens their world to new ways of learning. We look forward to cheering with you and picking out homeschool prom outfits and planning the resolution for the next value debate competition.

So what if that new homeschool parent isn't interested in the long haul? It happens. Homeschooling isn't always a permanent choice. We still encourage you and want you to have access to the very best tools and tricks, even if it's just until you move to your next home or your child finishes cancer treatment or you get off the waiting list for that brilliant new pre-K program. The rest of the tips in this book can help you. I wasn't always sure that homeschooling was forever for us either. While I'm now confident in my choice to stick it out, every family is different. The decision is, and should always be, yours.

TIPS FOR THE "JUST FOR NOW" HOMESCHOOLER

Temporary homeschoolers, also called short-term homeschoolers, have an extra challenge: giving their kids the best of homeschool while keeping them within certain targets that will be expected of them when they return to public or private school. While you may love the thought of letting your child lead their education with endless months of butterfly stories and trips to museums, you'll have to keep those milestones we mentioned in Chapter 5 in the back of your mind. As much as flexibility and freedom to pursue personal interests is good for kids (and the very reason why many of us homeschool), it can often be incompatible with how the school system assesses your child's progress.

That said, you'll still have plenty of freedom in many areas, such as when you teach your kid, what subject you teach first, how long they have to sit in one session, and whether they do school in the kitchen or the office. What they study, however, may be more circumscribed. Grade levels and curriculum choices matter more, too.

Embrace Standardized Tests

Regardless of how you feel about testing, you'll need to find a way to work it into your homeschool routine. Your state may not even require it, but the school you send your child back to will want to see proof that your kid is at grade level for their age before accepting them (especially if they've been gone a long while). Standardized tests are quite different from the quizzes and unit exams that are part of many homeschool curriculum options; if you want your child to be best adjusted for reentry into the school system, try testing at least once a year to keep your kid comfortable with how testing is done.

If your state already requires annual or periodic homeschool testing, they can usually direct you to their preferred testing tools. The school you hope to reenter may prefer one as well. Most of the common tests are available through homeschool groups or businesses that offer group testing for a fee. Some tests can also be ordered from homeschool supply companies to be administered at home by a qualified proctor. (In some cases, you may qualify.) Tests may be given via online or paper methods. The two most common include the Stanford 10 and the Iowa Tests. Some schools accept the ACT or SAT (and its PSAT counterpart) as suitable testing options.

Keep the Curriculum as Close as Possible

Some math and language publishers offer the same course materials for homeschoolers as they do for public and private schools. If your child will be enrolling in a private, faith-centered school, you'll likely be able to buy the materials they would use for history, literature, and religion courses. Buy the items closest to what your kids will be using in school and try to stay on track throughout the year at home. If they don't use something you can buy directly, find out what the benchmarks are for the grade level and work up to them independently with your own choice of materials. (Some schools make this information available upon request; if not, ask around. Parents whose children already attend the school may be willing to chat.)

Remember Extracurriculars

If it's possible for your child to participate in activities with the school or a group of peers from that school, look into joining as soon as possible. Whether it's sports, a band class, or an outside group like craft club at the library, any connecting point will help when it's time to go back to school. If your child was removed from school due to bullying or other issues and you don't want to maintain those connections, that's understandable. You may also be moving to a completely new district and don't have those relationships yet. Still, some kind of social, peer-related activity is recommended so that kids aren't overwhelmed when they return to the busy, noisy classroom after the (generally) low-key home experience.

LYNNAE'S STORY

Lynnae McCoy has three kids, ages twenty-two, seventeen, and ten, and has homeschooled when it made sense for her family, which wasn't all the time. She originally decided to teach her kids at home years ago because she wasn't happy with her local public school's budget cuts and their move to a four-day school week. She homeschooled her son until it became clear that he thrived in a classroom, so she put him in a private school for part of third and all of fourth grade. In middle school, he transitioned to public school before finding his place at a private school, from which he will have graduated by the time you read this book.

What did she do for the other kids? Her oldest daughter is autistic and needed the time at home to deal with social challenges in the middle school years. After taking some band and choir classes through the local public school, she regained the confidence needed to do well in school again. At her daughter's request, Lynnae allowed her to return to public school for her last two years of high school. The strong friendships her daughter had cultivated through these extracurricular activities helped Lynnae decide it was the right move.

Lynnae's youngest child started homeschooling for the first time during COVID-19. Lynnae's goal is to put her back in school once it makes sense for the family. In the meantime, she has enjoyed the ease and consistency of a boxed curriculum that focuses on geography, animals, and ecosystems—all topics that piqued her daughter's interest and would be fun to learn while at home. She did, however, choose a different math and spelling curriculum than what the boxed curriculum provider recommended—something more in line with the grade-level expectations of the private school she will eventually return to. A computer-based math program, which freed Lynnae from having to teach math, and a spelling workbook series ordered from Amazon fit her needs perfectly.

Lynnae demonstrates that it's possible to get the benefits of a boxed curriculum, such as lesson planning and easy-to-use teacher's manuals, while still exercising some flexibility for those other subjects that might be covered differently in public or private school.

WHEN TEMPORARY ISN'T

I was one of those parents who said I would never homeschool my kids. Then I tried it. Even at first, I was hesitant to call myself a "homeschooler," insisting that we would take it year by year and see how it went. But in truth, I was all in. For us, the reason was disenchantment with the educational offerings in our area. We were idealists trying to give our kids what we thought they deserved—and homeschool seemed like the only way to do it. But that's not everyone's situation.

Whether you consider yourself a temporary homeschooler or not, accept that this is your path for now, and be vocal about the benefits to help get your kids on board. Even if you hate the idea and are doing it only because of circumstances beyond your control, try to frame it as an opportunity for your children. Otherwise, they may pick up on your negativity and not learn in the way you hope.

Some parents find themselves reviewing the options year after year, until suddenly ten or more years have passed. Many don't ever go back to private or public school. These parents are often homeschooling's biggest advocates. But if you find yourself initially unable to relate to the cheerleaders of the movement, it's not just you! Find someone who was once reluctant or who is still on the fence. They're out there. You can chat and weigh the options together, without judgment.

Chapter 13

GETTING KIDS COLLEGE READY

not every kid is destined to go to college. For the homeschooler who's used to exploring all the options and finding the best fit for their kid, it's common to look at everything from entering the workforce immediately to trade school, apprenticeships, and working for the family business. But if a four-year college is in your kid's plans, don't worry—there's a well-trodden path there from homeschool. I didn't believe it myself at first, as there was so little direction on how to do it when I first started homeschooling. Now, with my oldest child set to graduate from a four-year private college around the time this book is published, I know that it's not only possible but not nearly as difficult as larger society might make it seem.

I can't cover everything in this single chapter, but I can share the basics. Use this as a checklist to help you stay on track as you get closer to the high school years, and again as you approach graduation.

KNOW WHAT YOUR FAVORITE COLLEGES REQUIRE

I've shared that I'm a fan of the eclectic method of homeschooling, and that our kids learn a little of this and a little of that, while still progressing toward larger goals. One way we made sure our daughter was ready to attend college was to look at the college entrance requirements and reverse-engineer our plans. In traditional school, it's common to not look at what colleges want until tenth or even eleventh grade, because most of high school is getting in those general credits that all students must take. Homeschoolers should consider starting this coursework as soon as the eighth grade to make sure you have time to fit it all in.

Make a list of likely schools for your child, even if they aren't ones they've expressed interest in. Pick some dream schools as well. Print out their requirements for application. Do they want three years of math or four? Are they requiring a foreign language? Do they consider Latin a foreign language? List all the minimum courses your child will need to fulfill the requirements. Start planning out what classes are likely to fill these from ninth to twelfth grades, with gaps for extracurriculars and specialized courses.

Next, see what standardized tests they prefer. They may state that they accept both the ACT and the SAT, but in reading further, you might see that they actually like the ACT better. (Forget what you've read about coastal schools preferring the SAT and midwestern schools preferring the ACT. There are no general rules.) There's also a new test in town, the CLT (Classical Learning Test), and it's made with classical homeschoolers in mind. Not every school accepts this, but those that do are eager to accept CLT high performers.

DON'T LIMIT YOURSELF TO ONE-YEAR COURSES

Many homeschool or curriculum publishers will sell subjects as one-year courses, but the truth is that some classes can be completed in much less time. Depending on your child's work ethic, you can finish one and a half classes (or even two, with summer months) in a year, giving you an advantage, or a chance to catch up if you're a little behind in math or science. I've known homeschoolers who want to do better on their SAT, so they've done both algebra I and geometry freshman year, using the summer to fit it all in. The same theory works for those who don't start algebra until sophomore year or later, due to learning difficulties or family health issues. If your child can keep the pace, don't feel that you have to limit coursework to what the traditional school environment plans for.

RESEARCH AND PLAN EARLY

High schools have guidance counselors who keep track of testing dates and college application deadlines and communicate those to the students. You don't have this luxury. While it may seem that you're at a disadvantage in having to look up everything yourself, you can in fact give your child a huge head start on testing and scholarship applications when you don't have to deal with the guidance office at all.

Did you know that:

- the CLT has a free eighth-grade version that helps kids practice, called the CLT8?
- Khan Academy offers free SAT prep that rivals anything offered commercially?
- the PSAT National Merit Scholarship Awards are open to homeschoolers in all fifty states?
- you can request test accommodations for kids with learning difficulties?
- some colleges offer scholarships just for homeschoolers?
- homeschoolers can schedule individual, private visits with nearly any college in the US?

There's a lot of info out there, and it's best to start planning early to get everything you need to help your kid reach the next step in their journey. Don't rely on your memory of how testing worked in your high school days (or even what your cousin's kid is doing now) to guide you on your child's college-prep path. Research, research, research.

TAKE EVERY OPPORTUNITY FOR TESTING

Do you remember taking the ACT or SAT as a high schooler? I remember so clearly waiting for the one date that my school held testing, and then breathing a sigh of relief that it was over. Today, high schoolers test more than once, and their high school may even host multiple tests during the year. Still, not every parent takes advantage of the many available testing opportunities. As a homeschooler, however, you can sign your children up for as many testing dates as you want, and they can attend them at most any high school in your area.

Studies show that students who took the ACT more than once had an average composite score that was 2.9 points higher than the scores of those who only took it one time.[1] That can be a considerable advantage in getting extra scholarship money or being put on the short list for a competitive school. In fact, 57 percent of ACT testers got a better score on their second test. While 22 percent scored lower the second time, colleges generally look at the better of the scores, so there's really no risk in trying again for a better result.

Homeschoolers have the flexibility to test when and where they want. This is something that students shouldn't ignore when looking for advantages in the college entrance game.

GET THOSE VOLUNTEER AND JOB HOURS IN

Homeschoolers are hardworking kids by nature, but they'll need to prove that they can handle the rigors of college by showing evidence of activities and employment. Many homeschoolers work for their parents in a family business, and this can be difficult to document as real work. (With parents filling the roles of teacher, superintendent, guidance counselor, employer, and activities director, you can see why colleges sometimes doubt the veracity of their children's lists of accomplishments.)

Try to set up outside volunteer and work experiences for your child, even if it's just a few hours here and there. Having a third-party "boss" who can write a recommendation letter is priceless. Consider everything from volunteering at summer camps to handing out boxes at the food bank as fair game for boosting your kid's extracurricular résumé.

DON'T PUT TOO MUCH ON THE GPA

The grade-point-average method of determining if a kid is college-ready has always been flawed. Being at the top of your class means different things in different schools, and it's easy to manipulate grade point averages as a homeschooler. This may be why, while colleges do consider GPAs, it's just one stat among many—including test scores, interviews, essays, and other credentials not influenced by Mom and Dad.

Most will ask for a transcript, however. You can create one yourself using any number of free online tools, or you can order one from a professional transcription service. Some colleges require that the transcript come from a third party; even though you put in all the numbers, they still need it to pass through someone else's hands to be "official." I think this is slightly unnecessary and just another cost to tack onto the homeschool budget, but it's not difficult to do.

FINDING A HOMESCHOOL-HAPPY COLLEGE

If your child has always been homeschooled, college may be the very first place where they're in the minority. My daughter didn't know any other homeschoolers at her school, but her professors were delighted with her performance. Aside from the initial culture shock (which shouldn't be too bad if they've been participating in group activities all along), there shouldn't be much difference between your child's college experience and any of her peers'.

However, some schools may hesitate to accept homeschooled students at all. The only way to really know if a college is homeschool-friendly is to see how they approach your child during the application process. And if you know any alumni or current students, ask around.

Most schools have, by now, updated their application pages to tell you exactly what they need from your child as a homeschooled applicant. But this doesn't mean they will "get" your child. There are still places that may assume these kids are ignorant or know social skills only from Mom and Dad.

If you're concerned about choosing a homeschool-friendly college, look for those that cater specifically to homeschooled children. Check home education magazines to see who's placing ads, or attend a homeschool conference and listen to what the speakers say. Ask other homeschooling parents where their kids go. You'll probably see a pattern, and maybe it will encourage you to check these schools out. But remember, even if your child ends up being a pioneer at their chosen school, there's nothing wrong with that. Someone has to be the first; if your child is prepared, they can excel in any environment.

{ *Chapter 14* }

FREQUENTLY ASKED QUESTIONS

How do you fit in hobbies, passions, and other pursuits while homeschooling?

I've been writing for over thirteen years, and while most people don't question that I can get a day's work in while homeschooling the kids, I did raise some eyebrows when I shared with my friends that I had completed my first, as-yet-unsold full-length novel.

"I wish I had the time to write a book" was the phrase I kept hearing again and again. People seemed to think that I had more time in the day than they did—that raising six kids and having a full-time career and maintaining several gardens and performing caregiving duties for my ninety-two-year-old grandmother were all things that somehow moved aside so I could have magical free time to write that book.

That free time didn't exist. I had to make it. Rather, my husband made it.

Remember how I shared that we've been tackling our homeschool literature list by reading to the kids every night? Without fail, for the entirety of our marriage, my husband has been doing read-alouds with our children every night. From the Chronicles of Narnia to all of Roald Dahl's books (yes, even *The Witches*), he was keeping a consistent tradition alive that helped our kids relax and unwind, bonded them to their father, and gave me twenty minutes every night to myself.

I used that time to write creatively.

I wrote that first novel over three years. Some nights, I got in a mere hundred words. Others, I was on a roll, and knocked out over a thousand words in twenty minutes, and promptly fell asleep from the exhilaration and exhaustion. It was my catharsis, my creative outlet, my way of expressing myself. Those twenty minutes were fiercely protected against text messages or the dog's whimpers to be let outside. My husband knew how precious those moments were, and he protected them, too.

You may not want to write a novel. But what could you do with that time? Learn a new language on an app, unwind with some fancy tea and a foot spa, or catch up on all those movie trailers you can't watch in front of the kids? Whether you use it to pursue a noble cause or just to check out for a bit, be sure you find some time every day to do something for yourself. It can make a huge difference in maintaining your identity and your sanity.

My always-homeschooled child has become obsessed with certain aspects of public school. Is this normal?

It's common for kids who have never been to a public or private school to be curious. When my daughter, who had never been to public school, was about nine, she started challenging our homeschool decisions. She insisted that she would be happier in public school, and we took the time to sit down and ask her why she thought so. It turns out that she was watching a lot of Disney Channel shows set in high schools. She had formed an opinion about what public school offered by the short interactions the teens had in front of their brightly painted lockers with all their personal belongings inside. They talked about life, love, and problems, and it was this experience of chatting about boy crushes while reaching for snack foods that intrigued her.

Once we determined that what she was looking for wasn't really found in a public school (few schools I know of have these pristine lockers and twenty minutes to stand in front of them while munching on chips), we were able to better meet her needs. We added some storage space to her bedroom and hosted a sleepover with her close girlfriends. It was never really about school. Take the time to listen to your child, but recognize that the experience they're picturing probably isn't accurate. Kids (like adults!) will occasionally suffer from "the grass is always greener" syndrome, and you should be prepared to meet that head-on throughout their educational years.

How can I help my children socialize?

You have to be careful using the "s-word" (socialize) around homeschoolers. Why? For years, all we heard from friends and family after sharing our decision to home-school was the dreaded "How will they socialize?" Most of these people were well-meaning, but a few have used the socialization question to argue that home education is ineffective. Hence the "awkward homeschooler" trope.

Before I explain some of the best practices we've used to help our kids learn healthy social skills, let me share this eye-opening statistic: In 2012, 91 percent of homeschoolers surveyed by the NCES cited a "concern with other schools' environments" as the most common reason for home-schooling. These parents specifically mentioned "safety, drugs, or negative peer pressure" at schools as part of that concerning environment.

Of course, your children will have plenty of opportunities to facilitate positive peer relationships, as long as you make some arrangements. Kids are naturals at making friends. Barring any developmental delays (which can be a significant challenge, no less in school than at home), they will usually find that one kid at the park they can chat with. As long as kids are placed in a safe and friendly environment where the parents share common goals and the kids are given a chance to explore and connect on their own terms, they'll be fine.

So, how can you develop these environments? Lucky for you, they already exist. Think of all the hobby-based groups available at public schools, such as sports teams, chess club, band, political interest groups, volunteer opportunities, and art classes. These all exist for homeschoolers. While the availability in your immediate geographic area may vary, I guarantee if you're determined to drive a bit out of your way, you'll find something great.

Admittedly, more introverted children may need a gentle nudge to "go talk to that boy over there with the same video game T-shirt," but it will happen eventually. Also, do it often and early, as soon as kids can participate in group activities for twenty minutes or so. Waiting until sixteen to introduce your child to a peer group will do them no favors. As a parent, you must take the initiative to help them learn and grow; their becoming a polite, productive member of society is all on you.

I don't understand why I would pull my kids out of public school just to put them back into the same types of sports and activities they participated in before. Isn't this just replicating the problem?
I can't speak to why you decided to homeschool. The stats show a wide range of reasons for families to disengage from institutional learning environments. One parent may decide that they've had enough of their child's daily exposure to drugs or violence; others may want to teach a history curriculum that more accurately reflects their own ethnicity or culture.

You're correct that if you pull your kids out of your public school's math and science classes only to put them right back into some of the shared learning experiences, you may not escape any of the problems you've tried to leave behind. I can also tell you that some homeschoolers try very hard to provide a parallel universe for their children that mirrors the milestones of public school. (There are graduations, field trips, spelling bees, and even proms.)

Are these "homeschoolized" versions of public school perfect? No. Are they different? Very.

Let's take prom, for example. In the public school setting, it's organized by a teacher or admin and put on with help from the students. It's chaperoned by teachers and sometimes a parent or two. The after-prom activities may be sponsored by the school as well. Some schools may have a parent-teacher group do much of the heavy lifting, but in the end, the school sets the rules and deals with any infractions. Parents may or may not have a say in how issues are handled.

In the homeschool prom world, it's the parents who decide the location, collect the fees, set the dress code, and plan the after-party. Parents chaperone. Parents enforce the rules. If you, as a parent, don't agree with the prom rules, you can take your issues to the group. They may or may not listen, but, ultimately, parents are responsible. No one gets to say, "I had no idea my kid did these things because it was the school's problem."

Parental control and responsibility are key factors in

pulling off a successful homeschool event. They aren't always perfect; homeschool kids can do bad things, too. But when they do, no one can blame anything on teachers, the school, or someone else's kids. We're all in this together.

We live in a rural area or a place far away from an organized homeschool "hub." How can I get my kids connected to other homeschoolers?

I know this dilemma well. We live forty-five miles away from the largest homeschool hub in our state, but it might as well be a thousand miles. By the time we get everyone loaded up for an activity, I get my business work set aside, we participate in the activity, and then get everyone home again, the day is gone. How many days do I truly have to walk away from my business and home duties? If I make all that effort to get a whole day off, I would much rather hit the lake!

One way we've managed to give our kids lasting friendships is through fewer meeting-intensive activities. Where a football team may meet three times a week for practice, plus games on the weekends, speech team may gather only on Monday mornings, with meets during competition season. This works much better for us with our schedule, and by picking something like speech, where kids ages ten to eighteen can all participate, we're making one trip as a family to connect all the kids at once. Sports, on the other hand, may have a separate team practice and game schedule for every age and stage; with six kids, we just can't do that. Your mileage may vary!

Summer camps are also a great way to help your kids learn and grow in ways that don't disrupt the regular school year. Whether it's a three-day camp or a monthlong experience, camps can be a great connection point. Many of my children's best friends were met at summer camp; they stay in touch via social media and video chats.

If money is tight or you just can't justify sending your kid away for very long, a learning intensive might be a better fit. These day camps are put on by universities, nonprofits, education groups, and sometimes even private companies, covering everything from geology to pottery to robotics. Kids connect with each other while also pursuing their passions; many of these friendships nicely subvert parental fears about peer pressure, as they support and cheer for one another to achieve skills and win competitions. (Many learning intensives are just one day, but some will offer overnight accommodations for out-of-towners at a discount. Parents are often encouraged to stay as well.)

My kid only wants to play video games. Is this harmful, and how can I promote socialization through this?

If your child is coming to homeschooling after a period in the public or private school system, video game binges may just be a normal part of their "deschooling" transition. Still, there will come a time when enough is enough, and hard boundaries will need to be drawn on how long they game and when it's appropriate.

That said, I don't believe video games (as a category of

entertainment) are harmful. They can help your child learn important social skills, such as teamwork and prioritization, if done in a healthy context. Here are some ways your child can get their gaming fix while also making friends:

LAN parties: Whether you have your kids join one that's been planned in your community or you create one with a group of like-minded homeschoolers, these get-togethers are a unique way for kids to game together. You'll want to take some precautions to ensure the internet connections are secure and that kids know the rules for interacting online, but *Minecraft* LAN parties are just one way for even younger gamers to hang out and share a common interest. (Do a search for how to host a LAN party to get ideas for forming a safe gaming environment; while homeschoolers are just dipping a toe into this world, I think it will really catch on in the next few years.)

eSports clubs and competitions: Did you know that many colleges are starting to offer scholarships for students who commit to playing competitive video games? If your child has the knack for it, encouraging an eSports hobby can not only help them use their gaming skills for healthy interaction and problem-solving development but also net them some cash for college. eSports is a significant time commitment, so do your research before you encourage your kid to try out. If they're going to play anyway, it might be nice if they make some real-life friends and connections.

The next time they want to play, ask if any of their friends will be online. Ask questions about what they're into. Get to know the people your children game with. The more local, in-person connections they can move into their online world, the better. You'll also have to accept that this is just how kids communicate these days, so while it might seem foreign to us, it's an important social outlet for many of them.

You should also try some of the games they play. There's a big difference in the gameplay between a first-person shooter and a building game like *Animal Crossing*. I've seen entire families (parents and kids) forming teams in these online worlds. Knowing the perks of each game and the relational benefits they may provide can help you explore the ways they can contribute to your child's growth. You can't speak of things you don't understand. Even if you don't see yourself gaming as a hobby, trying it out will bring you closer to your child.

Help! My child is easily distracted. How do I help him or her stay on task?

This is a super-common issue that parents have, and not every family is dealing with the same definition of "distracted." First, there could very well be an underlying health or wellness concern that should be addressed to help you have the best chance forward. Assuming this has already been done, however, there are some things that have worked for homeschooling families:

1. Set reasonable expectations for your child's attention span. When you sit them down to work, are

you breaking up tasks in ways that are appropriate for their age and developmental stage? Research shows that the average attention span for a four-year-old is no more than twenty minutes.[1] Think about that. A healthy child cannot even begin to sit for the time many school activities and pre-packaged homeschool lesson plans are demanding of them. Could you be making your homeschool more age- and development-appropriate to give them the very best chance of success? Try chunking up work into smaller sessions and use the real-family schedule and planning examples in Chapter 5 as a reference for the total number of hours a child should be doing formal learning. Adjust as needed.

2. Make sure you know what "distracted" really looks like. Some of the activities we associated with distractedness have been recently discovered to be helpers in focus and productivity. Doodling, for example, has been shown to help kids retain information better.[2] If you treat doodling as a help by providing your child with a notebook and pen during lectures, the problem is now reframed in a way that it's a solution. If you're very sure that your child is losing the ability to stay on track, however, move on to some focus tools.

3. If your child has sensory processing needs or any number of other issues that can affect their ability to be calm and focused, search out tools that the professionals use. Harkla is just one company that's making these solutions affordable for average families, and they offer everything from weighted blankets and lap pads to compression vests, sensory swings, and body socks. You may have to try out a few different things before you find what works. Homeschooling is a continual learning process, but the good news is that there are more solutions available than ever to support you and your family!

4. Finally, get in touch with homeschoolers who share your specific challenges. There are online groups aplenty for everything from sensory disorders to ADHD to kids who don't have any diagnosable issues but need constant encouragement to stay on track. Remember, unless you're seeing focus issues consistently, day in and day out, it may just be time to take a break. Distractions can be your child's way of saying "Enough is enough!" Put down the pencils and get outside for a nature walk or snuggle on the couch with a book. Kids are human, and just like grown-ups, they often lack the means of communicating when they need a change of pace. Listen

to them closely, and you may be surprised at how some of the focus problems work themselves out.

With more electronic schooling options available, how much time should be dedicated to non-electronic learning?

This goes back to what I discussed in Chapter 1 about virtual school vs. homeschooling, but I don't believe you can (or should) try to replicate an in-person classroom experience through digital methods. I'm a firm supporter of distance learning tools, such as live online courses, self-paced video offerings, software, games, and audiobooks. I also think all of these things should be done in moderation. Children who are made to sit for the equivalent of six to eight traditional classroom hours while parked in front of endless Zoom video conferencing sessions will not thrive. I can barely get through a forty-five-minute business meeting without mentally checking out; how can we expect it from a seven-year-old?

Experts have weighed in over the years on how much "screen time" kids should get, and even they've had to revise their standards after it became apparent that all screen time is not created equal. I believe the same approach should be taken to digital learning. It's not all the same, and setting a hard time limit may not work for you and your family.

Our family uses an approach where we allow one hour

of screen-time learning for every two hours of offline learning when kids are very young. Little kids should be playing with crayons and cardboard boxes first, then using their learning apps as a reward or for downtime while Mom and Dad work. As kids get older, they'll likely get more screen time, but you'll have to feel out whether they're getting too much of it.

Signs that your kid is getting too much screen time include:

- headaches (which may also be a sign of vision issues)
- irritability when not on devices
- lack of focus or attention
- not remembering what they've learned
- inability to entertain themselves with offline activities without a struggle
- sleep disruptions

While I could say that kids shouldn't get more than X hours of educational screen time, I know that many high-quality live learning platforms may require a bit more than that. You also have homework research (done online) and the typing of papers (more screen time). The best I can offer is to break up the screen work as much as you can and cut back on unnecessary digital entertainment during the more robust periods of screen learning. Kids need a break. Use your gut instincts to know when they need to pull back, and don't ever feel that you have to sit through hours of Zoom video or online live sessions. The point of homeschool is to make it work for you. If your kid is bored out of their mind with digital learning, change to something else. There's absolutely no reason to continue doing something that doesn't work.

What kind of relationship should you maintain with the local school?

This is an interesting question, as many of my homeschool peers have come to homeschooling after an uncomfortable or even unsafe situation at a school. When you withdraw your child under such circumstances, of course the relationship with that school might be strained; words may have been exchanged.

However, I think there's value in maintaining some ties with your local school. I strive to treat administration and teachers with respect in our interactions; that's just being a good citizen. But I haven't really had to interact much with them, coming to the superintendent only one time to sign off on a student work permit (something unique to Nebraska).

I, however, have never had my kids in the school system. We didn't have to disengage from programs or go through multiple parent-teacher meetings. My advice is to always be an advocate for your child, even if you have to bring in outside help (like a legal team or homeschooling organization) to get what you're entitled to under the law. With many states allowing homeschoolers to access public school resources, activities, sports teams, and IEP (Individualized Education Plan) tools, know your rights and don't be afraid to exercise them.

How do you prevent kids from accessing inappropriate content when doing online learning?

I'll answer this question with another question (sorry). What are you doing to prevent your kids from accessing inappropriate content while watching YouTube videos, playing online games, using social media, checking email, or listening to streaming music? If you answered "Nothing," you probably have a much bigger issue to resolve.

While there are numerous reports of "Zoom bombing" and other instances of inappropriate comments and content making their way into learning environments, the buck really does stop with you—the parent—in keeping your kid safe.

There are so many options on the market today to help monitor your kid's activity and keep them accountable to your family's expectations of using the internet. At a minimum, do the following:

- Set and list the rules for using the computer and internet-connected devices. When can they use them? Where in the home are they allowed? What programs do they have permission to access?

- Use the settings on your wireless router or another device to limit access in a way that makes sense for your family. This could mean turning off your son's wireless access to his phone after midnight or blocking everything but your online class URL during school hours.

- Add a monitoring solution, if possible. There are many on the market, and they range from passively sending you a list of places your children have visited to actually blocking anything you haven't whitelisted. Many of the major antivirus companies offer this as an add-on purchase or a free perk with a paid subscription.

- Speaking of antivirus software, you are using it, aren't you? If you're not regularly updating your security software and running checks against the bad stuff, stop reading this and do it right now. Malware and ransomware can do real damage.

Once you have your devices protected and the rules in place, you're still not done. Now discuss with your kids the dangers of the internet and what to do if they see something they shouldn't. It can be very concerning for a child of any age to run across some of the more unsavory things that have popped up online, from mature content to bullying; these issues should be talked about before they happen. In your conversations, you may learn that they've already seen things. Talk about it. Let them know you aim to keep them safe. Make sure they understand the rules, and the consequences if they break them.

Finally, most online learning environments are getting better about their security protocols, but mistakes are still made. You should have a secure login for classwork, and it should be connected to your child's account. Be wary of any program or software that allows guests to pop in without registering first. A good educational provider should have worked out the security issues so that your child can be safe while learning. If you don't see this happening, ask them, and don't be afraid to switch homeschool service providers until they get it taken care of.

How can I help my child adjust from public school life to the homeschool life?

It can be incredibly disruptive to a child to be pulled from school, even if the reasons are good and they're better off at home. Because it's such a big change, there will need to be a period of adjustment when you're patient and they're allowed to "deschool."

Deschooling is a term with two meanings. The first is a philosophy attributed to Ivan Illich that takes a poor view of schools in general and seeks to rid kids of the "toxicity" of the institutionalized school culture. I'm referring to the other meaning, which is essentially the period of adjustment a child goes through between regular school and homeschool. To "deschool" your child in this second way is to allow them time to get accustomed to the many changes and form a learning mindset again.

How do you deschool? Your child will likely act out or be stressed at least occasionally when making the shift, but these tips can help:

- Plan for a month or two of no formal schoolwork while the child adjusts. Read books, go on nature walks, watch documentaries, and talk about things the child wants to talk about.

- When the child has had some time to get their bearings, introduce one or two subjects a day to start.

- Schedule classes so that the more demanding studies are at the beginning of the day, when they have the most energy and focus.

- Check in often with your child and ask how they're doing. It's possible their issue is course-related, but more often it's a general feeling of loss or uncertainty due to the big changes they're going through.

If your child was pulled directly from public or private school in the middle of a school year, deschooling will be more apparent and will take longer. If you're starting fresh with homeschooling in the fall, use the summer months to get your child warmed up to the idea, and let them enjoy their time off!

One parent we interviewed had this to say: "If your children are young when you start to homeschool them, remember that you don't have to do school for as long as public school does. For early elementary, you may only do school for an hour or two a day, and that's just fine. Second, be flexible. Sometimes my kids just aren't ready to do school that day. Sometimes we take the day off, or sometimes I let them play and then pick up school in the afternoon. We homeschool year-round, so that gives us a lot of flexibility."

FINAL THOUGHTS ON YOUR HOMESCHOOL JOURNEY

These frequently asked questions were just a handful of over thirty questions I received when I asked my closest friends and family members what they would hope to learn from a homeschool book. Not surprisingly, the most common themes I heard centered on the question "How will I know that they're doing okay compared to other kids?" Keeping pace and showing progress seemed to be the biggest burden to new homeschoolers. No one wants to feel that they're allowing their kids to fall behind their peers.

Perhaps the most important thing to remember is to not compare yourself to other homeschoolers. It's hard. I do it, too. If you can focus on your child, their unique abilities and talents, and the progress they've made as individuals over the course of a day, week, month, and year, I promise you'll feel better about your role as homeschool parent. Home education works best if you can take advice when needed and keep your eyes on your own paper.

CONCLUSION

remember, like many people, where I was in early 2020 when I first heard of the novel coronavirus: in a hotel room, eating take-out sweet-and-sour chicken, missing my family, and working on a piece for a writers' conference I was attending. I felt there was something different about the news coming out of China, and that this virus might change things in a big way. Like everyone else, I had no idea how true that was.

Months later, as schools across the United States began to end early for the year—some moving to online formats, but many simply closing—I realized that homeschooling, my own family's lifeline for so many years, might also save the day for other families who had never considered it before. The disarray of patchwork reopenings and spotty remote learning was hard on everyone, but especially on children from already underserved schools and cities, or those with special needs. People were suddenly excited at the prospect of doing school in a new way. I was getting phone calls and emails from parents who saw this as their chance to break free from the existing systems and try education on their own terms.

Unfortunately, despite the new enthusiasm, our children's opportunities were narrowing. Museums, libraries, and sports complexes shut down. Social distancing restrictions made it difficult (if not impossible) for many of the things I enthusiastically shared with our homeschool-seeking friends to actually happen. The homeschool proms, family-friendly volleyball tournaments, field trips to the state capital, and cross-country park explorations came to a screeching halt. We were left, like so many other families, to make do with what we had in our own homes and backyards.

Even though we were better positioned than most to continue our kids' education uninterrupted, I grew frustrated by what we were missing. I worried about socialization and opportunities for employment and how this might appear on a college application years from now. I grew impatient with the world, as my work dried up (temporarily, thankfully) and trips got cancelled. Like every other parent on the planet, I wondered if I really knew what I was doing in the face of so many uncertainties.

One day in early November, I broke down. Things weren't where I'd planned for them to be. Nothing, from our budget to our family plans to our homeschool goals, was on track. After my long and passionate cry in the kitchen, my thirteen-year-old came to me, put his hand on my shoulder, and reassured me. He told me how lucky we were. He told me that this, of all the years we'd homeschooled, was the best ever. He told me how happy he was that we were all together in 2020 and he had family to be with and that I wasn't traveling as much or distracted as much or planning as much. He felt safe and provided for.

As it turns out, my kids learned a lot in 2020. Yes, they probably spent way too many hours playing *Destiny 2* on the Xbox, and they didn't get as far in their math as I'd hoped. And Latin? Don't get me started.

But my kids feel safe and valued. They're moving forward in the three Rs, and some other stuff, too. They've bonded in a way that I couldn't have imagined. They are, in the simplest terms, happy.

This spring, my oldest (and only) daughter, our original home-school "experiment," will be completing her bachelor of arts degree in media studies at an out-of-state private university. I'm looking forward to seeing her cross the stage for her diploma, but whether it's in person or through a live YouTube stream, I'll know that we certainly did our best.

And if, by some miracle, normalcy is actually restored this year, we may also get back to zoo field trips, ACT tests, and eight-hour drives to that little bakery in western Nebraska I've always wanted to visit. And if it isn't, I know that homeschooling has achieved what I originally set out for it to achieve: giving my kids the environment and opportunities to thrive as best as humanly possible in an uncertain world. Admittedly, preparing them for adulthood in this constantly shifting reality is hard, but I believe that, for many families, a home education can actually make it a little bit easier.

APPENDIX A
Resources

Chapter 3:
Homeschool Legalities and Requirements

Home School Legal Defense Association (www.hslda.org)

Google Drive (www.drive.google.com)

Apple iCloud (www.icloud.com)

Chapter 4:
Tools of the Trade

Institute for Excellence in Writing (www.iew.com)

The Pencil Grip, Inc. (www.thepencilgrip.com)

Kindle Fire Tablet and Amazon Kids+ (www.amazon.com)

Google Chromecast (www.store.google.com/product/chromecast)

Norton Antivirus (www.norton.com)

McAfee Antivirus (www.macafee.com)

Chapter 6:
Homeschooling through the Grades

Demme Learning (www.demmelearning.com)

Khan Academy (www.khanacademy.org)

Society of Health and Physical Educators (www.shapeamerica.org)

Nintendo *Ring Fit Adventure* (www.ringfitadventure.nintendo.com)

Math-U-See (www.mathusee.com)

Chapter 7:
Paying for Homeschool

Pinterest (www.pinterest.com)

Super Teacher Worksheets (www.superteacherworksheets.com)

LinkedIn Learning (www.linkedin.com/learning/me)

Khan Academy (www.khanacademy.org)

MOOCs (www.coursera.org/ and www.edx.org)

Chapter 10:
Working Outside the Home

Cozi (www.cozi.com)

Chapter 13:
Getting Kids College Ready

ACT Testing (www.act.org)

SAT and PSAT Testing (www.collegereadiness.collegeboard.org/sat)

CLT Testing (www.cltexam.com)

APPENDIX B

Sample Junior High and High School Course Outline

Science

Seventh Grade: General Science

Eighth Grade: Physical Science

Ninth Grade: Biology

Tenth Grade: Chemistry

Eleventh Grade: Physics

Twelfth Grade: Anatomy, Advanced Chemistry, Organic Chemistry, or similar

Math

Seventh Grade: Pre-Algebra/General Math

Eighth Grade: Algebra 1

Ninth Grade: Geometry

Tenth Grade: Algebra 2

Eleventh Grade: Pre-Calculus

Twelfth Grade: Calculus 1 or Math Elective

English

All grades (7–12) any of the following: Composition I, Composition II, Journalism, Creative Writing, British Literature, American Literature, or another creative writing or lit appreciation course

Social Studies

All grades (7–12) any of the following: World History, American History, History of the Culture of Your Choosing, Philosophy, World Religions, Geography, Religions of Your Choosing, Civics, Economics, Constitutional Law

Languages

Two years in high school of any language, including Latin, American Sign Language, Spanish, Italian, or other

Electives

Four years of any of the following: Art, Art History, Film, Music, Band, Dance, Computers, Programming, Psychology, Moot Court, Speech, Value Debate, Sports, Health, or other

NOTES

CHAPTER 1
Who Are the Homeschoolers?

1. "School Choice in the United States: 2019," National Center for Education Statistics, n.d., https://nces.ed.gov/programs/schoolchoice/.

CHAPTER 4
Tools of the Trade

1. Andrew Pudewa, "Convert to Pens!" Institute for Excellence in Writing, n.d., https://www.iew.com/sites/default/files/article/fileattachment/convert_to_pens.pdf.
2. 2. "Kids Need Stronger Parental Oversight Online," Center for Cyber Safety and Education, n.d., https://isc2-center.my.salesforce.com/sfc/p/#G0000000iVSt/a/0f000000fyoc/TYQ9XvDATBA78rR00G.PGJ9fmaLm1vQfAW9HCpy3GWk.

CHAPTER 5
Sample Schedules and Proper Planning

1. Sal Kahn, "Daily Schedule for School Closures," Khan Academy, accessed July 27, 2020, https://keeplearning.khanacademy.org/daily-schedule.

CHAPTER 6
Homeschooling through the Grades

1. Grover J. "Russ" Whitehurst, "New Evidence Raises Doubts on Obama's Preschool for All," Brookings, November 20, 2013, https://www.brookings.edu/research/new-evidence-raises-doubts-on-obamas-preschool-for-all/.
2. "Whole Language," *Wikipedia*, n.d., https://en.wikipedia.org/wiki/Whole_language.
3. Jean Soyke, "Math Mastery vs. Spiral Math," Demme Learning, March 24, 2016, https://demmelearning.com/learning-blog/mastery-vs-spiral-the-debate-continues/.
4. "Shape of the Nation: Status of Physical Education in the USA," Shape America and American Heart Association, 2016, https://www.shapeamerica.org//advocacy/son/2016/upload/Shape-of-the-Nation-2016_web.pdf.
5. US Department of Health and Human Services, *Physical Activity Guidelines for Americans*, 2nd edition, Washington, DC, 2018.
6. Virginia Clinton, "Reading from Paper Compared to Screens: A Systematic Review and MetaAnalysis," *Journal of Research in Reading* 42, no. 2 (May 2019): 288–325, https://doi.org/10.1111/1467-9817.12269.

CHAPTER 7
Paying for Homeschool

1. Brian D. Ray, "Academic Achievement and Demographic Traits of Homeschool Students: A Nationwide Study," *Academic Leadership: The Online Journal* 8, no. 1 (Winter 2010), https://www.nheri.org/wp-content/uploads/2018/03/Ray-2010-Academic-Achievement-and-Demographic-Traits-of-Homeschool-Students.pdf.

CHAPTER 13
Getting Kids College Ready

1. Matt Harmston and Jill Crouse, "Multiple Testers: What Do We Know About Them?" ACT.org, 2016, https://www.act.org/content/dam/act/unsecured/documents/2016-Tech-Brief-MultipleTesters.pdf.

CHAPTER 14
Frequently Asked Questions

1. Dr. Colette Poole-Boykin, "Homeschooling During COVID-19: Why All Kids May Not Need Eight Hours of Instruction a Day at Home," *Good Morning America*, March 25, 2020, https://www.goodmorningamerica.com/family/story/parents-teachers-tips-homeschooling-covid-19-kids-hours-69774140.
2. Srini Pillay, "The 'Thinking' Benefits of Doodling," *Harvard Health Blog*, December 15, 2016, https://www.health.harvard.edu/blog/the-thinking-benefits-of-doodling-2016121510844.

ABOUT THE AUTHOR

Linsey Knerl is a mom of six who has been homeschooling since 2004. Her interest in small business and entrepreneurship led to a freelance writing career that complemented her own home-school style. Linsey has been a trusted source for families since 2008. Her tips for budgeting have appeared in various publications, including *Time, Shape, Better Homes & Gardens, Reader's Digest, Family Circle, All You,* and *Woman's World.* Her media company (Knerl Family Media) has grown to include her better half in life and business, Sam. Together Sam and Linsey work to educate and support their growing family.